# M
## is for Misogyny

# M is for Misogyny
## Tackling Discrimination against Women and Girls in Primary School
# Sarah Wordlaw

§ Sage

1 Oliver's Yard
55 City Road
London EC1Y 1SP

2455 Teller Road
Thousand Oaks
California 91320

Unit No 323-333, Third Floor, F-Block
International Trade Tower, Nehru Place
New Delhi 110019

8 Marina View Suite 43-053
Asia Square Tower 1
Singapore 018960

Editor: James Clark
Production editor: Rabia Barkatulla
Marketing manager: Lucy Sofroniou
Cover design: Wendy Scott
Typeset by: KnowledgeWorks Global Ltd

© Sarah Wordlaw 2026

Apart from any fair dealing for the purposes of research, private study, or criticism or review, as permitted under the Copyright, Designs and Patents Act, 1988, this publication may not be reproduced, stored or transmitted in any form, or by any means, without the prior permission in writing of the publisher, or in the case of reprographic reproduction, in accordance with the terms of licences issued by the Copyright Licensing Agency. Enquiries concerning reproduction outside those terms should be sent to the publisher.

**Library of Congress Control Number: 2025939487**

**British Library Cataloguing in Publication data**

A catalogue record for this book is available from the British Library

ISBN 978-1-0362-0930-8
ISBN 978-1-0362-0929-2 (pbk)

# Contents

*Dedication* vii
*About the Author* ix
*How to Use This Book* xi
*Acknowledgements* xiii
*Introduction* xv

| | | |
|---|---|---|
| Chapter 1 | What is Misogyny and Where Do We See It in Schools? | 1 |
| Chapter 2 | How Can Leaders Develop an Anti-Misogynist Culture in Schools and Classrooms? | 17 |
| Chapter 3 | What Does a Feminist Curriculum Look Like? | 31 |
| Chapter 4 | Positive Masculinities | 49 |
| Chapter 5 | Social Media and Online Safety | 61 |
| Chapter 6 | Working with Parents and Carers | 77 |
| Chapter 7 | Working with the Wider Community | 91 |
| Chapter 8 | Suggested Lesson Plans and Topics | 105 |

*Appendix* 125
*Index* 131

# Dedication

This book is dedicated to all the incredible women in my life – strong, sensitive and smart – the brilliant girls I have the privilege of teaching and the bright and shining futures ahead of them. May they stand firm, shine bright and express themselves free from threat or fear.

And to you – a reader – thank you for taking the time to create space for change, challenge thoughts and commit to a more equitable future for *all* children.

# About the Author

**Sarah Wordlaw** is a headteacher working in South London and the author of *Time to Shake up the Primary Curriculum* (Bloomsbury, 2023). She writes extensively on curriculum reform and development, and diversity and inclusion, coaching leaders across the country and delivering CPD. Attention to the relationship between intersectional identities and privilege and the lived experience of pupils is at the core of her practice, ensuring that all children reach their potential, are safe and are able to navigate an ever-changing world as advocates for themselves and others.

## Reference

Wordlaw, S. (2023) *Time to Shake up the Primary Curriculum*. London: Bloomsbury.

# How to Use This Book

The purpose of this book is to create space for educators to consider a) the quality of your current curriculum offer, b) how it can be further developed to actively eliminate misogyny and c) how to further develop safeguarding practice in primary school through the lens of misogyny. In a period of turbulence and fundamental shifts in how we understand gender equality and safeguarding it is important to remember that real change is a marathon not a sprint. Real change comes as a result of careful auditing, planning and a collective will towards a shared goal.

This book is a significant practical guide for school leaders and those who aspire to leadership. It will act as a toolkit to identify first steps and to plan long term, as well as provide a step-by-step guide in first analysing the current curriculum. From there it provides a comprehensive guide to developing the different areas of the curriculum and practices and setting a whole-school strategic approach.

This includes ensuring a well-rounded feminist curriculum, including learning about and celebrating women's achievements through history and around the world, and associated role models. It includes learning about and from women from the global majority, Queer women and women with disabilities, challenging white and heteronormative bias across the curriculum. It includes teaching boys the concept of strong allyship, understanding consent, providing space to critique gender stereotypes and how to develop good mental health and expression of emotions for all children. This book supports teachers to use these areas to teach social justice, human rights and develop children's voices to articulately self-advocate. Developing voices supports children to speak out against misogyny and ultimately reduce violence towards women and girls.

There are also links to places to develop teachers' subject knowledge within each section.

Note: In this book you will find reference to Black peoples with a capitalised "B". This is because "Black" is understood as a political identity, representing a shared history, culture, identity and experience, whereas "white" as a general descriptor does not have the same unifying connotations.

# Acknowledgements

I am deeply grateful for the endless support of my wonderful partner, her patience, knowledge and unwavering belief in me and her understanding as I dedicated countless hours to writing [and talking about] this book. I also want to thank my dear friend Marie for her inspiration for the front cover – creative as ever!

# Introduction

> 'Violence against women is perhaps the most shameful human rights violation, and it is perhaps the most pervasive. It knows no boundaries of geography, culture or wealth. As long as it continues, we cannot claim to be making real progress towards equality, development and peace.' Kofi Annan (UN, 1999)

The purpose of this introduction is to present and explain the context of misogyny, both the international picture and then the national context. It will include key definitions of terms and statistics which describe the societal backdrop educators are working within. It is important to first understand the context, as this helps to get to grips with how we can make a change to our everyday practice, policy and curriculum.

Misogyny is a form of extremism, and must be addressed now. Official statistics tell us that in the UK in 2023 a woman was killed by a man every three days. With violence against women and girls on the rise – especially post-Covid – now is the time for educators to step in and use their sphere of influence to work towards eliminating this ongoing violence to stop misogyny. Misogyny is a dislike of, contempt for or ingrained prejudice against women. This is a safeguarding issue which affects all, irrespective of their gender. The word has evolved to encompass the more widely held attitudes and behaviours that relegate women to subordinate positions and maintain the power imbalance which characterises male/female relations. To quote the final report of the Working Group on Misogyny and Criminal Justice in Scotland: 'It is these attitudes – and the conduct which flows from them – which prevent us achieving genuine equality' (Kennedy, 2022).

I want to be really clear from the outset about how we classify women and girls. In this book, when the term 'women' is being explored, this is a trans-inclusive definition. Women and girls are any persons who live and identify as female though they may have been said to have a different sex at birth.

Misogyny and violence against women and girls remains a real issue within our society, so it is extremely important we address it in schools and that we start early. Violence against women and girls (VAWG) is the name given to the different forms of violence experienced disproportionately by girls and women because of their gender, including domestic violence, forced marriage, 'honour'-based violence, female genital mutilation (FGM), rape and sexual harassment.

In a 2024 report by the organisation End Violence Against Women, it was found that:

- 68% of the public believe more should be done by the government to tackle violence against women and girls
- 50% of the public do not trust the police to tackle violence against women and girls
- 46% of the public do not trust schools in tackling sexual abuse occurring on site

In Laura Bates' *Fix the System Not The Women* (2022) the author explains how in the UK an average of one rape per day on school premises is reported to the police, with nearly a third of secondary-aged girls reporting sexual assaults at school, from other students. An astonishing 90% of girls report receiving unsolicited sexually obscene photos and a further 92% reporting sexist name-calling. There are also numerous reports of girls having their photos taken without consent – this is evidenced in The Everyday Sexism Project, an online catalogue of the everyday experiences of sexism from the 'outrageously offensive or so niggling and normalised you don't even feel able to protest' (Bates, 2012). There are countless experiences of girls being told to change their uniform – wear longer skirts, shorts under skirts, long sleeves, etc. – as it may be distracting to their male counterparts. This is an example of the systemic blame put on women's bodies being the problem, when the real problem is the shame and sexualisation of the female body by a historically patriarchal society and the lack of respect afforded to women and girls generally. Beyond this, girls speaking out about these issues has often led to them being reprimanded for using their voice, disciplined and/or labelled as difficult. When we add in other factors such as race into the equation, it gets even more disturbing, for example labelling a Black girl as 'aggressive' for speaking out against blatant misogyny and violence. Unfortunately these experiences are a microcosm of what is happening in our wider society. If the policies and practices of the school are reinforcing misogynistic standards, how can we ever expect to teach boys to recognise problematic behaviours and act in a way to eliminate violence against women and girls? If this is the experience of girls at secondary school, it is even more important for educators to ensure that tackling misogyny at primary school is at the forefront of learning and practice.

Guidance from the PSHE Association (2023) on addressing misogyny explored how women and girls in particular are put at risk by narratives which promote unhealthy relationship behaviours, victim-blame and normalise sexual abuse and harassment. It describes how toxic gendered stereotypes can be deeply damaging to children's view of themselves, but also how they treat others. This ranges from developing insecurities about body image and agency to normalising abuse and violence against women and girls. Strong PSHE education is crucial for safeguarding and building resistance to problematic narratives. Both boys and girls (and everyone in between) are victims of sexism, misogyny, and toxic masculinity.

Teachers play a huge role in developing seismic shifts in inclusive thinking in society. This book aims to act as a guide for teachers and leaders on what we can do about misogyny at primary level and guides teachers to teach more inclusively so that children learn to be happier individuals and more well-rounded citizens. It is research-led, evidence-based practice, which stems from the view that curriculum is a key pillar of preventative safeguarding practice. A book like this is needed *right now*, to develop subject knowledge, practice and awareness to prevent further increase of misogyny within our young people.

## Definitions and Language

Words are powerful and support us to navigate, understand and challenge the world around us. Definitions and understanding of ideas are ever-changing as we learn more and more so it is important that we are really clear about our definitions before going any further. Here are some of the key terms and ideas that will be explored in this book, and their definitions.

*Discrimination*: Unjust treatment of a person or group of people, on the basis of a particular category, typically but not exclusively race, sex, disability, ethnicity or age

*Femicide*: The killing of a woman by a man

*Feminism*: Advocacy of women and girls' rights, aiming for equality of the sexes and genders

*Gender*: The characteristics applied to men, women, boys and girls which are socially constructed, including roles, norms and behaviours associated with each. As this is a social construct, the idea of gender can vary over time and between societies

*Hyper-masculinity*: The idea of hyper-masculinity is the idea of exaggerating stereotypical 'manly' behaviours in order to be seen as 'a man'

*Intersectionality*: Describes the interconnectedness of the social categories that make up a person, typically but not exclusive to race, gender, disability, ethnicity, class, religion, etc.

*Incels*: An online community of men, who are hostile towards women because they feel they are are unable to attract a woman – a portmanteau for involuntary and celibate

*Misandry*: Hatred, extreme dislike of, or prejudice against men and boys

*Misogyny*: Hatred, extreme dislike of, or prejudice against women and girls

*Patriarchy*: The name of the system and/or government where men hold the power, where power between men and women is unequally distributed to the detriment of women. It refers to the historical system that 'has been designed by and for those who have always held the most power in our society: white, wealthy, non-disabled men' (Bates, 2022)

*Sexism*: Stereotyping or discrimination on the basis of sex

*Stalking*: This behaviour may include: regularly following a person; attempting to contact, or contacting, someone by any means; repeatedly going uninvited to their home; monitoring/checking someone's internet use, email or other electronic communication; deliberately loitering around somewhere they know the person often visits; watching/spying on a person; interfering with someone's possessions

*Violence*: Behaviour of physical force with an intention to hurt or damage

*Woman*: A person who identifies as female, regardless of their assigned sex at birth

# International Context

Globally, nearly one in three women – or around 736 million women aged 15 or over – have been the subject of physical violence or sexual violence at least once in their lifetime (UN Women, 2024). Because of this, the rates of anxiety and depression disorders, HIV, unplanned pregnancies and sexually transmitted infections and many other health problems are much higher in women who have experienced violence. Fifteen million teenage girls from 15 to 19 years old globally have experienced forced sex (UN Women, 2023). Around the world, approximately 200 million women and girls between 15 and 49 years old have experienced female genital mutilation, with one in four women experiencing it in sub-Saharan Africa (UN Women, 2023).

Pycroft (2022) describes gender-based violence towards women and girls as an international issue, happening in every society globally. In 2020, 81,000 women and girls were killed globally, with 58% of those deaths being at the hands of a family member or partner, averaging one woman's death every 11 minutes (Pycroft, 2022). Unfortunately the number of gender-based killings is on the rise, particularly after the pandemic – more people at home, more violence and killings within the household and more women and girls being unsafe with their partners and/or family members. If we then hone in on Western Europe, the increase in killings has been around 11%, more stark than the increase in South America and southern Europe both at 5% and North America at 8%. Furthermore, research shows that a quarter of women aged 15– 24 years old who have been in an intimate relationship, will have experienced violence from that partner by the time they reach their mid-twenties. This evidence is even more significant when you consider that this reflects only the *reported* violence, and that it is suspected much gender-based violence goes on in homes unreported. A further statistic shows that nearly half of women who have experienced violence in their homes globally have not reported it to anyone, nor sought help. Even fewer women consider reporting this violence to the police, indicating a global mistrust of the systems designed to keep us safe. When you consider that globally an average of 15–20% of police officers are female, this is explained somewhat (Pycroft, 2022).

In a UN global study on gender-related homicide (UNODC, 2018), it was found that the continent with the highest number of women killed by an intimate partner or family member was Asia (20,000 women), with Africa a close second at 19,000 and then the Americas at 8,000, Europe at 3,000 and finally Oceania at 300. Despite this, it was found that Africa was the continent where women ran the largest risk of being killed by a family member or intimate partner (UNODC, 2018).

## Intersectional Identities

Delving into the lived experience of women with intersectional identities (or positionings) that may put them at a disadvantage or lead to discrimination, the statistics are even more worrying. Intersectionality is essential when understanding the context of VAWG and how this intersects with other forms of societal discrimination like racism, gender identity, homophobia, transphobia, ableism and classism. This means for some women that they experience double the oppression, othering and in some cases extreme eroticising of their bodies and sexuality. This is particularly the case for Black women. The global Black Lives Matters protests in 2020 illuminated the deep impact of systemic racism, and highlighted the disappearance and murder of numerous Black women such as Nicole Smallman and Bibaa Henry (Selvarajah, 2021). There was little to no coverage in mainstream media because they were Black women and the BLM movement acted to bring their deaths to society's attention. In addition, women who are migrants, Black and other global majorities and those who are neurodivergent and/or disabled are more vulnerable to violence and less likely to have sought support (or in seeking support have not been believed or received appropriate help).

Looking at the experience of LGBT identities and people's lived experience of violence against women and girls, the National LGBT Survey found transgender people are more likely to experience physical threats or sexual violence. Eighty eight per cent of transgender people do not report the hate crimes they experience, and of the small number who did, 48% were not satisfied with the response from the police (Stop Hate, 2024). A research project run by SafeLives found that both transmen and women are referred to services for domestic abuse at a similar rate, both were extensively more likely to have a male perpetrator than female, showing that controlling behaviour and physical abuse were the highest forms of domestic violence (Catch 22, 2022). In addition, there are numerous barriers that LGBT people face when seeking support services, examples of which being trans identities being used against survivors/victims like deliberately forcing gender performance outside of the survivor/victim's indeed and or incorrect use of pronouns. Furthermore, not having visible inclusivity within support services causes many within the LGBT community to seek support elsewhere, or not at all (Catch 22, 2022).

## Me Too Movement

The Me Too Movement began in 2006, when the phrase 'MeToo' was used by American Tarana Burke, an activist who wanted to raise awareness around the prevalence of sexual assault and abuse within society. Fast forward to 2017, the hashtag #MeToo was used on social media to show the great magnitude of women who have been sexually assaulted and raped. It was also used to demonstrate solidarity and strength in numbers. The movement is global and survivor led, a way to call to action, fight for justice and create healing pathways for survivors of sexual violence. The MeToo movement recognises the impact of the pandemic on women's safety, particularly at home and that isolation caused many women and girls to feel trapped in unsafe home environments, cut off from resources, support and help.

There are many activists in Africa doing brilliant work around sexual violence such as Kadiatou Konaté who is disrupting Guinean society, and other women speaking out in francophone African countries such as Ivory Coast, Senegal, Guinea, Cameroon and Benin. Activities face the threat of physical violence for calling out the attack on women's bodies. In Senegal, where rape has only been criminalised since 2019, the hashtag #balancetonsaïsaï, created by feminist Ndèye Fatou Kane and meaning 'out your rascal', was used to call out a series of femicides and rapes in 2018. In 2020, journalist Bintou Marian Traoré started the hashtag #vraiefemmeafricaine ('real African woman'), which many people consider the francophone #MeToo movement, which was used as a parody on the idea of the 'authentic' African woman. The climate of violence puts these francophone African feminists at serious risk of harm but they persist due to the number of requests for help they get from women in need. Chanceline Mevowanou, a social activist from Benin said 'To overcome the embryonic stage of feminism in French-speaking Africa, we must put our efforts into education from an early age in order to dismantle systemic oppression at its roots. Without that, there will be no real feminist revolution' (Kane, 2022).

## National Context

The National Police Chief's Council UK commissioned the national policing statement for violence against women and girls, finding:

- Over one million VAWG related crimes were recorded during 2022/23, accounting for 20% of all police recorded crime.
- Police recorded VAWG related crime increased by 37% between 2018/23.
- At least 1 in every 12 women will be a victim per year, with the exact number expected to be much higher.
- Child sexual abuse and exploitation increased by more than 400% between 2013 and 2022. (NPCC, 2024)

This demonstrates that not only is violence against women and girls increasing, but there are ever more complicated types of offending causing significant harm to victims and furthermore society as a whole. One sixth of murders in the UK we related to domestic abuse in 2022/23, with 'suspected victim suicides following domestic abuse rising year-on-year' (NPCC, 2024).

In Harriet Johnson's 'Enough' (2022), the author notes that 50% of women surveyed in 2021 feel unsafe walking by themselves, at nighttime, near their home (compared to 17% of men). This is even more the case for disabled women who felt more unsafe and furthermore 20% felt unsafe leaving their homes during the *daytime*. This is no way to live. A report in 2018 noted that nearly three quarters of parents surveyed told their daughters not to walk home in the dark, or even to go to certain places. It's the culmination of these changes to female behaviour in the name of 'safety' which result in the shrinking humanity and freedom felt by women and girls (Russel and Southgate, 2018).

It is impossible to discuss the national UK context of violence against women and girls without mentioning Sarah Everard and Sara Sharif. Sarah Everard was walking a short distance home one evening, when she was kidnapped, raped and murdered by a Metropolitan Police constable, in March 2021. The perpetrator, Wayne Couzens, who had used his warrant card to get Sarah into his car, had an extensive history of alleged sexual offences. This case, unfortunately one of many, highlights the dangers faced by women and girls, daily. A poll in 2021 found that 50% of men surveyed after Sarah Everard's murder said they'd change their behaviours like walking on the other side of the road from a woman in the dark so that she feels safer and stepping in if a woman is being harassed (Johnson, 2022). Whilst this is seen as a positive reaction, it shouldn't have to be a horrific rape and murder which prompts this.

Sara Sharif was a 10-year-old girl who allegedly died at the hands of her father, stepmother and uncle, after facing over two years of abuse at home. Sara had numerous injuries all over her body such as bite marks and burns. This is the awful story of a child being abused at home, allegedly known by extended family members and no one acting upon seeking help for this girl. When she was found, she had 11 spine fractures, burns caused by an iron, a traumatic brain injury and 'probable human bite marks' (Fuller and Wilkinson, 2024). This demonstrates that home is not a safe haven for all children.

Domestic homicide is on the rise, specifically femicide, with post-Covid Home Office figures showing 49% of women killed in the home were killed by their intimate partner, with over half of the male perpetrators being already known to the police for previous domestic abuse. Furthermore, of 854,734 reports of domestic abuse in 2021, only 77,812 referrals were completed, with only 54,515 prosecutions made (End Violence Against Women, 2022). This suggests that asking for help in most cases does not result in help, support or prosecution, so many women would feel that there is little point in reporting this type of crime.

When we look at the national context through an intersectional lens, we find even more disturbing results, with women who are more marginalised within our society disproportionately facing more violence and abuse. The proportion of global majority women being victims of domestic homicide was on a 15-year high post Covid, and the barriers to support and protection are indicated by the fact that these women are less likely to be known to police and other agencies (End Violence Against Women, 2022). Black women in London are more likely to face femicide than other ethnic groups. Information from a number of police forces between 2016 and 2020 showed disproportionate outcomes from the criminal justice system, a perpetrator being 1.5 times more likely to be charged if the victim was white rather than Black, demonstrating deeply rooted stereotypes around assumed victim/survivor credibility. Data also shows that mixed race and Black adults are more likely to experience sexual assault than either white or Asian adults (End Violence Against Women, 2022).

Disabled women experience a higher rate of domestic abuse than non-disabled women – this could be from an adult family member or a partner. Research also shows that disabled women are twice as likely to be a victim of rape and sexual assault (Safe Lives, 2024). That said, data from multiagency risk assessment conferences (MARACs) shows that only 3.9% of referrals were for disabled women (Safe Lives, 2024). There is a gap here between what is reported and what is actually happening, further demonstrating the lack of safety many disabled women experience in their homes. Marac data shows that only 3.95% of referrals for MARAC were from disabled people contrasting with the SafeLives recommendation of 16%+. Disabled people are more likely to be living with the perpetrator, deeply affecting feelings of safety and ability to report. In addition, disabled women face larger barriers to justice and protection because of deeply harmful stereotypes which often infantilise their competency, especially when giving evidence. Furthermore, the Equality and Human Rights Commission suggested that disabled women are further disadvantaged by remote video-link court hearings (Selvarajah, 2021).

If we then look at data for the LGBT community, specifically trans women, we see similar patterns of disproportionate violence and lack of justice from the criminal justice system. In 2023, hate crimes against transgender people in the UK were up by 11% from the previous year (Goodier, 2023). Of course, transphobic rhetoric contributes to this rise of awful hate. According to Goodier's findings, in 2023 hate crimes towards transgender people were significantly less likely to result in a court summons or charge (Goodier, 2023).

## The State of Women's Healthcare

Female health discrimination is rife in the UK, with the gender health gap the largest amongst the G20 countries (ITN, 2024). This is not new – the gender health gap has been prevalent for centuries. 'Health gap' describes the differences in 'the prevalence of disease, health outcomes, or access to healthcare across different groups. The gender health gap describes the sexism within healthcare, and the poorer service and outcomes women receive as a result' (ITN, 2024). Less than 2.5% of research funded publicly is put aside for reproductive health, despite a third of all women in the UK suffering from a gynaecological/reproductive health issue. Premenstrual syndrome (affecting 90% of women) receives five times *less* research than erectile dysfunction, which affects only 19% of men (ITN, 2024). Part of the discrimination against women is that women's health issues tend to be normalised and dismissed – those who suffer with period pain (premenstrual dysphoric disorder – PMDD), endometriosis, menopause symptoms – the list is endless – are told to get on with it and advised to take a paracetamol. This of course is dangerous – both physically and mentally. Physically it means women suffer with pain unnecessarily and in some cases die earlier, and emotionally it means they are gaslit into thinking that what is hurting them is not a big deal. Again, within this total dismissal of women's health issues is the lived experience of marginalised groups within the wider group of women – global majority women are less likely to be included in the little research that is taking place. Long-term conditions such as anxiety, hypertension and osteoarthritis are seen three times more in Black women than white women and Black women are nearly four times more likely to die after childbirth (Kaur Takhi, 2023). These experiences of Black women are a result of a history of systemic racism within the UK, resulting in them experiencing both race-based discrimination and misogyny – or 'misogynoir', a term coined by Moya Bailey, a Black feminist writer (Bailey, 2022).

## Online Misogyny

In a world where children are accessing social media from a younger and younger age, we need to get our heads around understanding the growing beast that is online misogyny. Harmful content and ideologies are quickly normalised online through algorithms on social media, meaning that children can be exposed to extreme content easily. Clicking on or liking what might seem an innocuous post, can lead to algorithms which expose children to echo chambers of the same and increasingly more violent or disturbing misogynistic content. Quite quickly, a child's entire feed can be curated with harmful content, meaning children could be engaging with dangerous individuals without even knowing it.

In 2021, almost 95% of 3–17-year-olds were using some sort of video sharing platform (VSP), the key ones being TikTok and YouTube, despite many being under the minimum required age (Internet Matters, 2024). Some of the ideas and ideologies around misogyny are simply becoming part of mainstream culture – key influencers and content creators such as Andrew Tate are well known. Such influencers – inordinately rich and seemingly carefree – often show their lavish lifestyles, which many impressionable children may aspire to. Hatred of women and girls is promoted in various online communities that promote the idea that women are inferior to men and should be treated as such. These ideas can be found in images, videos, comment sections and forums and can range from subtle to overt, name-calling to vulgar content. The online organisation Internet Matters (2024) found that by nine years old, 10% of children have seen pornography and this increases to 27% by age 11. Online pornography exposes children to normalised, harmful and oftentimes extreme misogyny and behaviour towards women and girls and warps understanding of healthy relationships. Much pornography online celebrates and promotes a man's dominance over a woman, often in increasingly violent ways, and shows women 'enjoying' abuse. With children getting personal devices younger and younger, the doors are being opened for children to access this damaging content from younger ages. Children may also be less likely to ask a trusted adult questions about it because of feeling embarrassed (Internet Matters, 2024).

## Incel Culture

Incels – or involuntary celibates – are an online subculture of men with a dangerous and highly misogynistic belief system. The movement started in 1997 for people struggling to find love and meaningful romantic relationships but has evolved into something much darker now, where women are objectified and dehumanised in a triangle of entitlement, jealousy and misogyny (Van Brunt and Taylor, 2021). Incels are men who feel genetically inferior to other men and feel they cannot compete for the love of a woman. Men who are incels experience depression, isolation and alienation. That's not to say all men who are depressed are incels; rather, most men who are incels are depressed. There is an extensive incels dictionary with vocabulary running from disrespectful to outright misogynistic. Incels meet online, through the 'manosphere' (an online network of men with harmful misogynistic views) and use their shared language to discuss collective injustices and grievances, and in some cases plan violence and attacks upon women (Van Brunt and Taylor, 2021).

# Gender Stereotypes – Beyond the Pink and Blue

Gender is a social construct used to describe the roles and behaviours associated with what is understood to be a woman, man, girl or boy. Cordelia Fine (2011) describes it as being 'flexible, malleable and changeable' with the majority of differences between the genders being socially constructed rather than biological differences. Gender stereotypes are outdated and harmful yet still highly prevalent within our society. Fine subscribed to the idea that men and boys have to be strong, and to be strong is not to show or express emotions, that women and girls must aim to please, be obedient, not outspoken and take pride in unobtainable – and often obscene – beauty standards. The impact of these gender stereotypes on children is one which deeply and negatively affects mental health, self-esteem and body image to name a few. Those who do not conform to these stereotypes often suffer even worse mental health. These stereotypes often limit confidence in girls and sometimes create over-confidence and aggression in boys. They are reinforced by society through the colour of clothes and types of toys. Gender stereotypes limit the ambition of our girls and limit the expression of boys – both of which are highly damaging to children.

The idea of hyper-masculinity – the 'norms' that make up what it means to be a man, to be manly – in itself is very damaging. A survey in 2018 found that 61% of young men aged 18–24 expressed they felt pressured to show 'hyper-masculine' behaviours in challenging situations, with 55% saying they felt they could not cry in front of others as this is not a 'manly' behaviour and 53% saying that they felt it was not OK to ask for help (Johnson, 2022). This works towards creating a tempest of mental health decline, loneliness and anger which is damaging in a number of ways. It is no surprise that with these statistics, male suicide in the UK is three times higher than female suicide and that most (85%) violent crimes are committed by men (Johnson, 2022). If we use this lens to look at our boys in primary school, we really need to critique gender stereotyping, develop our understanding of mental health and when it's OK to ask for help and teach allyship from the get-go.

## In Summary ...

Make no mistake. Misogyny is a global emergency which needs to be addressed now. This is a problem for all of us – irrespective of our gender. This is not a women's issue. This is a *human* issue. As primary educators we must act now; we have an opportunity to make a real difference to the safeguarding of children and to make the next generation safer than ours.

The aim of this book is to equip educators with tools and practical advice on how to create safety for boys and girls (and everyone in between). It works on the following assumptions:

- Misogyny is a *safeguarding issue*
- Misogyny is *a trans-inclusive issue*
- Misogyny is an *intersectional issue*, disproportionality affecting those who are most marginalised by social factors
- Girls must feel safer and be equipped with *self-advocacy*
- Boys must develop as *strong allies*
- Strong mental health, empathy and altruism will support children *to be safer*
- We can *make a difference* to the safety and wellbeing of future generations

# References

Bailey, M. (2022) *Misogynoir Transformed: Black Women's Digital Resistance*. Blackstone Publishing.

Bates, L. (2012) The Everyday Sexism Project. https://everydaysexism.com

Bates, L. (2022) *Fix the System, not the Women*. Simon & Schuster.

Catch 22 (2022) 16 days of action: LGBT+and gender-based violence. www.catch-22.org.uk/resources/lgbt-and-gender-based-violence

End Violence against Women (2022) Violence against Women and Girls: Snapshot Report 2021–22. www.endviolenceagainstwomen.org.uk/wp-content/uploads/EVAW-snapshot-report-FINAL-030322.pdf

End Violence Against Women (2024) Violence Against Women and Girls: Snapshot Fourth Edition. https://www.endviolenceagainstwomen.org.uk/wp-content/uploads/2024/02/Snapshot-report-Feb-2024.pdf

Fine, C. (2011) *Delusions of Gender – How Our Minds, Society, and Neurosexism Create Difference*. W.W. Norton & Company.

Fuller, C. and Wilkinson, H. (2024) Sara Sharif hooded and burned by abusers – court. BBC News. www.bbc.co.uk/news/articles/cn8jnggdj0qo

Goodier, M. (2023) Hate crimes against transgender people hit record high in England and Wales. *The Guardian*. www.theguardian.com/society/2023/oct/05/record-rise-hate-crimes-transgender-people-reported-england-and-wales

Internet Matters (2024) What is misogyny? www.internetmatters.org/issues/online-hate/what-is-misogyny

Johnson, H (2022) Enough. The Vioelence Against Women and How to End It, William Collins

Kane, C. (2022) Francophone African feminists forge their own #MeToo movements. *Le Monde*. www.lemonde.fr/en/le-monde-africa/article/2022/10/11/francophone-african-feminists-forge-their-own-metoo-movements_5999866_124.html

ITN (2024) Women's health in focus: Closing the UK gender health gap. *ITN Business*. https://business.itn.co.uk/womens-health-in-focus-closing-the-uk-gender-health-gap

Kauer Takhi, S (2023) Misogynoir in healthcare: Reviewing the 2023 Women's Health Strategy. National Suvivor User Network (NSUN). www.nsun.org.uk/misogynoir-in-healthcare-reviewing-the-2023-womens-health-strategy

Kennedy, H (2022) Misogyny – A Human Rights Issue, The Scottish Government, p8 https://www.gov.scot/binaries/content/documents/govscot/publications/independent-report/2022/03/misogyny-human-rights-issue/documents/misogyny-human-rights-issue/misogyny-human-rights-issue/govscot%3Adocument/misogyny-human-rights-issue.pdf

NPCC (2024) Violence Against Women and Girls (VAWG) National Police Statement 2024, College of Policing. file:///C:/Users/wordl/Downloads/National%20Policing%20Statement%202024%20For%20Violence%20Against%20Women%20and%20Girls%20(VAWG)%20-%20July%202024%20WEBSITE%20PUBLICATION.pdf

PSHE Association (2023) Misogyny, online influencers and the PSHE curriculum. https://pshe-association.org.uk/guidance/ks1-5/misogyny-online-influencers-and-the-pshe-curriculum

Pycroft, H. (2022) Violence against women: The statistics around the world. Action Aid. www.actionaid.org.uk/blog/2022/11/01/violence-against-women-statistics-around-world

Russel, L. and Southgate, J. (2018) Street Harassment: It's Not Ok, Plan International UK. Available at: https://plan-uk.org/file/plan-uk-street-harassment-reportpdf/download?token=CyKwYGSJ

Safe Lives (2024) Disabled people and domestic abuse spotlight. Safe Lives. https://safelives.org.uk/resources-for-professionals/spotlights/spotlight-disabled-people-and-domestic-abuse

Selvarajah, R (2021) Response to Home Affairs Select Committee's Call for Evidence on Violence against Women and Girls. End Violence against Women Coalition. www.endviolenceagainstwomen.org.uk/wp-content/uploads/FINAL-EVAW-response-to-HASC-VAWG-Call-for-Evidence-May-2021.pdf

Stop Hate UK (2024) About Hate Crime: Transgender Hate. www.stophateuk.org/about-hate-crime/transgender-hate

UN (1999) 'Violence against women 'most shameful', pervasive human rights violation, says secretary-general in remarks on International Women's Day. United Nations. https://press.un.org/en/1999/19990308.sgsm6919.html

UNODC (2018) Global Study on Homicide. www.unodc.org/documents/data-and-analysis/GSH2018/GSH18_Gender-related_killing_of_women_and_girls.pdf

UN Women (2023) Africa. Facts and figures: Ending violence against women. https://africa.unwomen.org/en/facts-and-figures-ending-violence-against-women-1

UN Women (2024) Facts and figures: Ending violence against women. https://www.unwomen.org/en/articles/facts-and-figures/facts-and-figures-ending-violence-against-women

Van Brunt, A. and Taylor, C. (2021) *Understanding and Treating Incels*. Routledge.

# 1
# What is Misogyny and Where Do We See It in Schools?

'I would like to ask that we begin to dream about and plan for a different world. A fairer world. A world of happier men and happier women who are truer to themselves. And this is how to start: We must raise our daughters differently. We must also raise our sons differently.' Chimamanda Ngozi Adichie (Ngozi Adichie, 2014)

## Introduction

So, what is misogyny? As discussed in the Introduction, misogyny is defined as the dislike or contempt for, or ingrained prejudice against, women and girls. The definition can also include 'an aversion to women, bias against women or a belief that men are better than women. It can also refer to social systems or environments where women face hostility and hatred because they're women in a world created by and for men – a historical patriarchy' (Wiltshire Police, 2024).

This chapter will enable you to:

- Define societal behaviours which demonstrate misogyny
- Understand the scale of misogyny and sexism within UK society
- Understand gender inequalities that children may have been exposed to before they start school
- Pinpoint areas in which misogyny is seen in schools
- Audit the curriculum for anti-misogynist practice and plan for improvement

To understand what this looks like in schools we need to first look at how children might experience misogyny in society. Language is such a powerful tool – when we can name something, it becomes real in a more tangible way. Misogyny can manifest itself in many different ways, from the overt to the grim undertones that can be felt, but sometimes not explained or believed. It's often seen across the systems that are supposed to keep us safe – from healthcare to social care, to policing and education (and let's not get started on politics). It's the monster hiding in relationships (romantic, family and friends), lurking in some religious beliefs, and skulking around in our criminal justice system.

Here are just some examples of misogynistic behaviour and attitudes prevalent in our society:

- Objectifying women such as harassing, catcalling, stalking, staring, and taking pictures without consent of women and girls
- Expressing hatred for women and girls – in real life or online
- Belittling women or girls, such as using sexist nicknames or making derogatory remarks
- Favouring men at the expense of women and having double standards – one rule for men and one rule for women
- Rigid, limiting beliefs in traditional gender roles
- A belief that a woman or girl cannot do something because they are a woman or girl
- No respect or regard for women's time and effort in either social or professional settings
- Seeking to control women and girls' behaviour
- Coercive behaviours such as using humiliating or intimidating behaviour to break down a woman or girl's self-confidence and undermine her
- Ignoring or speaking over women and girls and rejecting women and girls' ideas
- Taking or stealing ideas from women but refusing to credit them
- Punishing women for calling out sexism, discrimination and violence
- Aggressive, threatening, violent or intimidating behaviour towards women and girls
- Sexual assault and rape

It is a difficult list to read because if you are a woman reading, you are likely to have experienced a number of those behaviours, and if you are not a woman, women you love *will have* experienced much on that list.

It is also impossible to talk about misogyny without exploring the idea of intersectionality, and how person's social and political identities lead to individual and layered lived experiences of privilege and discrimination. The lived experience of being a woman *and* Black for example, is different from the experience of being a white woman. The lived experience of a refugee woman in the UK will be different that of a woman born in the UK. These multiple systems of oppression interact with each other and these interactions shape a person's life and experience.

## How Children May Experience Misogyny

Let us now look at some contexts in which children may experience misogyny.

### Misogyny and Religion

Many traditions and dogmas of mainstream religions, particularly monotheistic religions, are rife with misogynistic views and practices – it's one of the things that many religions have in common. That's not to say that religion is inherently misogynistic. However, it is a fact that some religious practices can be misogynistic – from the subtle to the blatant. Many children are exposed to these beliefs from a young age and it may be woven into their daily lives. In some cases, there is harmful teaching that the marginalisation of women is acceptable, that female inferiority can go without challenge and that roles of leadership and authority cannot be occupied by women. It is important that we understand this so we can start to unpick it.

Sexual prejudice or 'the internalization of negative attitudes and cultural stigma toward sexual minorities' (Etengoff and Lefevor, 2021) is associated with some religious practices and beliefs. When we also look at the intersection of homosexuality and gender, many religions are less tolerant of homosexuality and gender equality (Etengoff and Lefevor, 2021). Etengoff and Lefevor also argue that misogyny, sexual prejudice and religious sexism are not an inevitable outcome of faith and religious practice – there are a multitude of other factors (such as conservatism and/or cultural factors) which contribute to this and ultimately this outcome happens through individual interpretation based on these factors (2021). In addition, many religions depict God as a man. This idea itself is not inherintly misogynistic; however, the idea that a higher spiritual authority is afforded to men but not to women is (Alba, 2019). Johnson (2015) discusses how Christian scripture, for example, uses almost exclusively masculine language for God such as Father, King, Son, Lord, which can lead to perpetuating misogyny even though Christian theology maintains God has no gender (Johnson, 2015). The idea that women are spiritually inferior is an extremely harmful idea which children are exposed to from a young age. Language can be easily weaponised or deliberately restricted in terms of gender to benefit the elite (the use of a 'male' God, as the absolute zenith of being, usurped for the justification or support for the promotion of a male lineage of ascension of Kings), allowing misogynistic interpretations and meanings to seep in with enormous ramifications. In schools we have to be aware of this and careful not to perpetuate harmful language misuse.

Other examples of misogyny within religion are the presentation of women as temptresses distracting men from the serious business of worship. An example from the Bible is Eve – the first woman – who disobeys God, going on to tempt Adam and bring about his downfall. There are some religions where females can hold senior positions, however they tend to be the exception, not the rule. There are many female Rabbis, however this is condemned by orthodox Jews. In the Roman Catholic Church, archbishops, priests, cardinals and the Pope are men. Many branches of Islam do not accept female Imams. This exclusion of women from senior positions exemplifies how women are marginalised in religious life. In addition, there are arguably misogynistic customs and cultures in some religious organisations where the freedom of women is restricted, such as rules regarding contraception and abortion as well as unequal directives around marriage and divorce. Some feminists see purdah adopted by various Hindus and Muslims – religious women being secluded from public and veil-wearing – as exemplifying patriarchal control and misogyny. These hold significant restrictions on the fundamental life choices for women which are not placed on men. Many early religions feature prominent female figures and goddesses – it is patriarchal society which have reshaped and reinforced misogynistic values (Gelling, 2022).

## Misogyny and the Media: Music, Film and TV

Punch and Judy is very much a thing of the past (and rightly so!). However, when we look at the media children are exposed to from a young age, through the lens of misogyny, there are some startling results. A 2019 research project into stereotypes in UK children's TV by Hopster (a commercial provider of media for pre-school children), found that whilst there are some improvements to representation within children's television, gender stereotypes are still rife. Most children have access to a TV, tablet or are able to watch content on an adult's mobile phone, before they start at school. The report found that the average under eight-year-old has around two hours of screen time per day, and that half of all three- to four-year-olds will have accessed content on YouTube (Hopster, 2019). It found the following gender stereotypes to be widespread, after analysing 50 UK children and toddlers' programmes:

- Male characters fighting to express emotion
- Males being the main bearer of all knowledge
- More male protagonists than female
- Many examples of image-obsessed female characters
- References to it being 'girly' to cry
- Boys depicted as troublemakers
- 'Chubby' and 'fat' women or girls being depicted as monsters
- Overly muscular male characters
- Females in job roles such as beauty therapists
- Portrayal of females as slim, long haired, big eyed with long eyelashes

As educators, it is not within our sphere of influence to amend children's screen time, but the knowledge of what they may be exposed to supports us to develop critical thinking around gender stereotypes and helps us to understand pupil behaviour more.

## Pinkification: Toys, Clothes and Books

Pink is for girls and blue is for boys seems like an idea lifted from the 1950s. However, it is still widely seen today. This idea limits children's interests and embeds gender stereotypes from an incredibly early age. T-shirts which say, 'little cutie' for girls but 'cheeky monkey' for boys are downright ridiculous and books targeted at specific genders such as 'Handwriting for girls' (I wonder which cursive words are more 'girly'?!) seem nonsensical. There is some great work being done on de-gendering clothes, toys and bookshops, with organisations like Let Toys Be Toys campaigning for companies to remove their signs labelling 'boys' and 'girls' sections. Despite this, even without the signs, many spaces are still highly gendered.

Gender differences in children's clothing goes beyond colour though and includes the throwback of female clothing having fewer/smaller pockets. This was initially the case in the 17th century when women had to wear their pockets underneath layers of underclothing such as petticoats, meaning pockets were generally inaccessible without taking off their clothes. Post the French Revolution it's rumoured that women's pockets were banished altogether because men were expected to carry the money and important items, while women looked after the home. Fast forward to the 20th century – women's clothing got slimmer and tighter, and the rise of the handbag meant women's pockets got smaller. Fast forward again to now and it is *still* the case that girls' clothing has fewer pockets than boys. This seems absolutely ludicrous and appears to suggest that girls should have less adventure, be less curious and have fewer treasures (rocks, toys, etc.) to carry around on their person, and that life should be less convenient for them.

## How Might We See Misogyny in Schools?

So knowing that children are entering school with many deeply ingrained ideas about men and women, boys and girls, how might this manifest itself within the school gates? Misogyny in schools is symptomatic of gender equality in society. By the time children start primary school, many will be self-selecting books, toys, friends and activities based on gendered beliefs. By the time they reach seven years old, many children strongly identify with their own gender and act on and conform to their understood gender stereotypes.

As we become more aware of the power of words and appropriate language, so too we become more aware of our choices as educators and the impact they can have upon the children in our care, shaping their view of themselves, each other and the world around them. It is critical to understand misogyny in schools so that we can work to promote respect between girls and boys and foster an environment of equality.

## Note

The challenge comes when sex and gender are confused. It is damaging to view gender as innate. Gender is a social construct and is not binary or fixed. It is complex and should be viewed more as a spectrum, with people identifying with different and/or multiple points. Women, girls, men and boys can relate to and have both male and female characteristics. In addition, there are also people who do not identify with the spectrum at all – this is referred to as agender. It should not prevent children – girls or boys – from engaging with or participating in an activity or making choices.

## Misogynistic Language

Misogynistic language, which undermines and insults women and girls is commonplace in schools, experienced by both children and staff. This creates an environment which is unsafe for girls and contributes to a wider context conducive to sexual harassment. Many practitioners may not have the confidence or knowledge to address the issue properly. Harmful language reinforces negative and narrow ideas about what it means to be a woman or man in society.

Exposure to misogyny and sexism as a child develops discriminatory attitudes in the future and limits ambition. It is greatly harmful to children – particularly girls' self-esteem, self-worth and confidence.

## Examples

Language which refers to negative female characteristics:

'Throw like a girl'

'Don't be a pussy'

Language which focuses on superior male characteristics:

'Man up'

Language with is sexually gendered:

'Slag'

'Whore'

In some situations, what is considered 'low-level' sexist language or 'banter' can often be tolerated in a way that overlooks its profound effects.

It can also be seen in the language used by adults around the school: by teachers, support staff, visitors. It is often unintentional, but the language adults use can perpetuate harmful gender stereotypes, reinforcing what it means to be a boy or a girl.

## Examples Around School

How adults address other adults or children: 'sweetie', 'mate', 'man', 'ladies'

Asking children to help with jobs: 'I need some strong children to help me' and then picking predominantly boys

Making assumptions about professional roles: 'Yesterday I went to see the doctor.' Reply: 'What did *he* say?'

---

### Tip! 1.1

Ask yourself, how is sexist language logged? Is sexist language treated with the same severity as racist and homophobic language? Get your team together to do an analysis of the language used when reporting incidents and see if any trends appear.

---

## Gender Stereotyping

Gender stereotyping happens when a person is expected to act in a certain way based on society's expectations related to their gender: strong, aggressive, non-emotional boys and kind and quiet girls.

## Curriculum

Representing women and men in the curriculum is an extremely important way to dispel gender stereotypes. Historically, men have dominated in many fields of study in national curriculum subjects. The examples of artists, composers, explorers and inventors that we expose children to are often men – specifically white men. It is important to ensure that children are exposed to a range of role models from a variety of different genders, races, ethnicities and classes.

Likewise ensure that reading spaces are representative of an active effort to challenge gender stereotypes with the characters, themes and topics. In children's picture books, you are more likely to see a male protagonist than a female one, even to this day, and it is more likely that there is a male villain than a female one.

---

### Tip! 1.2

Look through the books in your book corners and school libraries and see how many books perpetuate or challenge gender roles. You may find some relics whilst searching – you don't necessarily need to get rid of them, just think about how you could use them – for example, in a PSHE lesson *about* gender stereotypes. Make a list of the texts you have which challenge gender roles so you can keep track of them in each classroom.

---

## Classroom Environment

Classroom interactions caused by the environmental set-up can reinforce gendered expectations and behaviours. In many classrooms, girls are used almost as a behaviour management tool, whose seats are chosen on the basis of behaviour rather than learning. Without explicit classroom rules – for example for talk – more dominant characters tend to take over discussions and navigate the classroom talk and learning. Think carefully about how your seating plan is organised and secondly how children are encouraged to voice their thoughts and challenge others respectfully.

## Behaviour Management

In the UK, boys have over 1.5 times the rate of suspensions than their female peers and are twice as likely to be permanently excluded (DfE, 2024). Educational psychology research (OER, 2024) found incredibly interesting points on teacher behaviour management and the language inadvertently used. They found that whilst teachers interacted with both sexes reasonably equally, there were differences in the content and public visibility of those interactions. In classrooms where boys are more assertive and loud, they tend to receive more of the teacher's attention, whereas if there are quieter children, they have less interaction with the teacher. This doesn't come as a surprise but what is interesting is that teachers tend to have a greater physical distance when speaking with boys, compared to girls. This could be for a number of reasons. One explanation is showing a more nurturing attitude towards girls than boys. Another could be that in more male-voice dominated classrooms the interactions are less personal and more public. There are also interesting differences in the distribution of praise and criticism, with the main one being that boys are praised more for knowledge whereas girls are praised more for compliant behaviour. This results in a feeling that for boys, knowledge is more important whereas for girls, it is behaviour.

In terms of managing playground behaviour, children are mirrors; they mirror the way an adult speaks with them. If during playtime, there is a physical altercation on the playground, and an adult shouts aggressively, 'What are you doing?', that adult is modelling exactly what you are asking children *not* to do. If we want to teach children to resolve conflict thoughtfully and empathically, we have to model it when we are managing behaviour ourselves. Pot kettle black and all that!

### Tip! 1.3

Reflect. Are there unconscious gender differences in the way you praise children? Ask a colleague to peer observe you and give honest feedback. Catch yourself when praising and see if you can spot any differences. Be mindful of the language used and what you are praising for!

## Playtimes, PE and Sports

Sport is still strongly connected to ideas of masculinity and is often made to feel important to the identity of boys. These stereotypes often go unchallenged in many different sporting contexts, from primary school PE to elite sports. It's important that staff members out on duty challenge sexist language and ensure that there is structure to playtimes, meaning that there is more than just football on offer. Children playing football also need support around winning, losing and challenging each other with kindness and avoiding a toxic level of competitiveness, which tends to be dragged into the classroom – affecting learning, often for the rest of the day! Staff members should be actively facilitating play (or even better, playing with the children themselves), modelling including others and great sportsmanship, positive language and congratulating others when they win.

Ensure that opportunities for sporting events are offered to a range of children, in a range of sports, and these are celebrated with an equal weighting in assemblies and the like.

## Everyday Practice

We often see gender stereotyping within everyday practice – unconsciously, in primary school. Think about jobs that you ask children to do – is it assumed that girls are more helpful and are therefore asked to help tidy up versus asking boys to do jobs such as moving furniture?

When you are doing quick grouping of children, is this done via gender – for example, in PE, 'boys are in team 1 and girls in team 2', or having different lines for girls and boys. In addition, there are also gender biases deeply embedded in uniform policies and many schools' uniforms still unnecessarily prescribe different clothing for boys and girls – an inclusive dress code allows children to challenge gender stereotypes and works to equal the field of what boys and girls can do, achieve, enjoy and express. Research has shown that girls with low body confidence can be put off from doing PE and sports because of concerns about how they look or feel in PE kit (NEU, 2024).

## Stereotype Threat

Stereotype threat describes what can happen when people are, or feel they may be at risk of, conforming to a stereotype. This can drastically affect performance in tasks both physical and mental, and academically. It is most likely to affect gender (or racial) minorities and it can result in disengagement, absenteeism and general unhappiness. An example of this may be girls feeling that boys are better at mathematics or boys feeling that girls are better at English, leading them to perform worse in exams.

# Auditing the Curriculum

Part of being able to tackle misogyny in primary school is fully auditing where you are now, then making a plan for change. This comes through auditing the curriculum, practices and subject knowledge. This cannot be done by one person but must be a whole team effort. Curriculum development must be part of the school's strategic plan complemented by rigorous professional development to support teaching and learning. Auditing first then planning for change means your practice is evidence led and research based. Your staff must be willing (and excited) to educate themselves on gender issues. Make sure you actively work to improve the staff's knowledge and literacy in this area. The better the staff knowledge, the more impactful curriculum development and practice will be. There are many ways to do this but most importantly, provide space and time for open and honest conversations, enable staff to speak freely about what they do and what confuses them, and be willing and open to respectful challenge. Staff will bring much relevant, valid and enlightened knowledge and life experience with them. You can also make various sources of information available to staff to help in improving their knowledge surrounding these issues, like books, articles, magazines, TV shows and documentaries and podcasts.

> **Tip! 1.4**
>
> Buy a lovely basket and put some books and magazines on gender issues and place them in the staff room. Staff can borrow books and it will also be a stimulus for meaningful discussions. You could also use QR codes to share links to podcasts and other media.

As our understanding of this matter evolves, so must our curriculum. Take time to think about what you want to achieve with your curriculum … to be able to self-advocate, to be strong allies of others, to keep themselves and others around them safe. Ask yourself, what does your current curriculum offer? How anti-misogynistic is it?

## Auditing Advice

1. Meet as a team (this could be senior leadership or the whole team) to make sure everyone involved is clear about the school's vision. This gives the audit direction and ensures everyone is on the same page. All work to tackle any gender imbalance must be considered as a whole-school issue, and all strands of gender imbalance must be tackled *together*. Diversity of thought is vital in completing an effective audit – you must have a range of staff with different experiences.
2. Auditing is as much about the *people delivering* the curriculum as it is the curriculum itself. All involved need to be willing to be honest, to challenge respectfully and to be challenged.
3. Remember – it is a marathon not a sprint. Effective auditing takes time; the process of gathering evidence should be thorough and take time. If you are a leader, put aside time for this. You could set aside several staff meetings so you are not giving staff additional work, and delegate different parts of the audit to different staff members. If you are not a leader, be sure to express your intended impact when you request time, for example, 'I would like to request time out to audit the curriculum so that it can be further developed in line with the school's vision, and ultimately improve safeguarding and outcomes for children.'

## Evidence Base for an Audit

- Whole-school ethos/curriculum statement
- Whole-school curriculum maps
- Year group curriculum maps
- Library and/or reading spaces
- Imagery around the school
- Trips, visitors and enrichment
- Pupil voice

- Staff CPD
- Lesson visits/observations
- Data, data, data! Assessment data, attendance data
- Policies: teaching and learning, anti-bullying, behaviour, safeguarding and child protection, etc.
- School website

## Test the Team's Unconscious Bias

We all hold onto biases, both conscious and unconscious. Unconscious bias is the unintended preferences we have towards certain people based on the associations we have with their individual characteristics. It describes the way we automatically respond – either positively or negatively – to others based on visible differences like gender, ethnicity, age and disability. It happens as a result of the external influences of the media, cultural norms, family and friends, school and education and lived experiences. It is important for practitioners to be aware of what their unconscious biases may be, so that they can be addressed. These biases can often be seen in interactions between pupils and teachers.

Ask each member of your team to take an unconscious bias test – there are lots available online for free. Tests work in different ways but often have activities including sorting words into different groups as quickly as you can. This is then followed by questions about your own beliefs, attitudes and opinions on gender-related issues. This provides practitioners with an interesting piece of data about themselves, and will hopefully allow for some self-reflection. If teachers are open to sharing feedback with the team, and there are whole-school trends in the practitioners' views, you can put together a CPD plan.

## Audit Questions

When auditing, you need to make sure you consider the school's strengths and weaknesses within each area. The audit questions below come from The Key (2023) Whole-school audit: gender and LGBTQ+ inclusivity.

Do teachers …

- Split pupils based on gender in the classroom?
- Use gender-based rewards based on gender (e.g. pink and blue stickers)?
- Use gendered expressions such as referring to groups of children as 'boys', 'girls', or individuals as 'sweetie', 'mate'?

Does the school environment …

- Have gender-segregated zones (for example boys' cloakroom)?
- Have gender neutral toilets?

- Have period support for pupils with periods (for example access to sanitary products)?
- Reading areas based on gender in book corners or school library?
- Represent a range of women's voices through display boards?
- Welcome all pupils to all areas – for example, girls to the football pitch?

Does the school facilitate …

- Equality groups led by students?
- Equal access to sports, clubs, PE and extra-curricular activities?
- Representation of women and discussions around women's rights outside of the specific national celebrations like International Women's Day?
- Trips to places which challenge gender stereotypes?
- Work with the parent community to encourage and support women's voices and inclusivity?

Do policies and practices …

- Explicitly state that sexual harassment is not tolerated?
- Explicitly have gender-neutral uniform, not listing trousers under boys and skirts under girls?
- Explain in code of conduct that assumptions should not be made about pupils based on gender?

## Pupil Voice Questions

Ask children …

- Do you feel safe in school? Why? Why not?
- What do you learn about keeping safe in school, at home, in the community?
- Do you feel heard in school? Why? Why not?
- Do you feel welcome in (add specific areas in the school – e.g. classroom, football cage, playground, library) Why? Why not?
- Do you enjoy learning at school? Why? Why not?
- Is there a trusted adult in school you could talk to if you felt you needed to?
- What do you do online (e.g. gaming, social media, chat to friends)?
- What do you learn about healthy friendships/relationships?
- What does consent mean to you?
- Is sexist or misogynistic language used at school?
- What have you learnt about body awareness, safe touch, body safety, the PANTS rule?
- What is it like to be a girl/boy at this school? Do you think there are any differences in experiences? (Be mindful of non-binary, trans pupils, gender questioning children.)
- What is school like if you are not a 'typical' boy/girl?
- What have you learned about gender stereotypes?

## Beyond the Curriculum

To get a fully rounded view of the school's practice, the key systems and processes which support the wider school vision should also be reviewed and audited. They include:

- *Recruitment processes.* What do your interview teams look like? Do they consist of men only or women only?
- *Policies.* Do all anti-bullying, behaviour, safeguarding and child protection policies contain a zero-tolerance statement about gendered harassment and sexist language?
- *Visible diversity in school displays.* What evidence is there, including intersectional identities – e.g. photos/pictures of people of different genders, sexualities, races, body shapes, religions?
- *Wider community events.* Are a wide range of people invited to run assemblies, career events, actively including female role models and role models from intersectional identities?
- *Toilets.* Are they gender friendly? Is there a gender-neutral option? Are there period products available?
- *Uniform policy.* This should be gender neutral in both its wording and application, and focus on health and safety rather than 'modesty' and first and foremost consider the comfort of the wearer. If there is a skirt as part of the uniform, there should be no skirt-length-rules as this perpetuates sexualisation of girls and victim-blaming, not to mention not taking into account different body shapes and heights. No modesty policing!

### Tip! 1.5

Don't do an audit by yourself. Bring your team in, allocate different elements of the audit to different staff members. For example, teachers could do peer observations, the PSHE lead could do pupil voice alongside a member of the senior leadership team (SLT), the curriculum lead could look at the whole-school curriculum, the English lead at the library and/or book corners. This process of auditing is likely to take a half term at the minimum, and likely two staff meetings, one at the start and one at the end of auditing, bringing all the information together and discussing what to do with it then.

## Plan for Improvement

Once you have a range of evidence, this will enable you to pinpoint your areas of improvement. For example, it may be that the curriculum itself needs development in terms of planned opportunities to learn about misogyny, or it may be that the curriculum is strong but staff practice demonstrates bias and the playground doesn't feel safe for girls. Discuss the evidence as a group and bring it together into an actionable plan.

> ### Tip! 1.6
>
> - Explain a clear vision and understanding of expectations when changing practices across the school
> - Delegate, delegate, delegate! Empower to step forward and take on implementation responsibilities, giving appropriate time and support to do this (and being mindful of workload)
> - Narrow your focus to a *specific* area of the curriculum for development, rather than every subject and every area, which is unmanageable. For example:
>   - Develop the representation of gender in books: library, book corners, on display
>   - Develop the teaching of masculinity, femininity and misogyny in PSHE
> - Your audit is your baseline measure – be sure to refer back to this when checking for progress
> - Allow enough time for the implementation cycle of improvement
> - Make fewer, but more strategic, implementation decisions and pursue these with greater effort

## Implementation Strategy – Cycle of Improvement

The Education Endowment Foundation (EEF) gives advice on effective implementation and explains that strong 'implementation is critical for turning engagement with research into tangible changes in school practices and pupil outcomes, including, crucially, for pupils experiencing socio-economic disadvantage' (EEF, 2024). Changing established habits and behaviours takes time and patience, and is a social process at heart, because change is as strong as the engagement of your practitioners.

Four steps of implementation:

1. *Explore*. Define issue, collect evidence
2. *Prepare*. Plan, plan, plan. Train staff, develop infrastructure
3. *Deliver*. Support team with expert CPD, monitor progress, adapt strategies. Include expert coaching, mentoring and well-structured peer-to-peer collaboration
4. *Sustain*. Plan to sustain and scale to ensure consistency, reward good implementation practices (EEF, 2024)

> **Tip! 1.7**
>
> Create a staffroom library and put some books and papers around this issue in it. At best, staff may find a paper or book to take home or dip into. At worst it will prompt a conversation. Here are some great examples:
>
> - Laura Bates, *Fix the System Not The Women*
> - Laura Bates, *Men Who Hate Women*
> - Cordelia Fine, *Delusions of Gender*
>
> *Note:* Be aware that you may have staff members who are personally affected by violence against women and girls. Always have your wellbeing services displayed and resources which signpost where staff can seek support if needed.

# In Summary ...

The audit tools in this chapter are a way of reviewing where you are now and helping you understand what the next steps are and which areas need more development, stimulating meaningful discussion and planning for improvement. Of course, the way you complete audits is up to you and what works best for your school and/or position. The most important thing is that there is a clear vision to set the purpose of the audit – otherwise it can feel overwhelming.

- *Who you bring to the table matters*. Ensure auditing is completed by a range of staff members within your team
- *It's a marathon, not a sprint*. Allocate time and space to audit and to plan for improvement. Be mindful of workload
- *Zoom out*. Auditing practice goes beyond the curriculum. Remember to zoom out and take into account wider school practices and policies for gender bias

# References

Adichie, C. (2014) Chimamanda Ngozi Adichie: 'I decided to call myself a Happy Feminist'. *The Guardian*. www.theguardian.com/books/2014/oct/17/chimamanda-ngozi-adichie-extract-we-should-all-be-feminists

Alba, B. (2019) 'If we reject gender discrimination in every other arena, why do we accept it in religion?' *The Guardian*. www.theguardian.com/commentisfree/2019/mar/06/if-we-reject-gender-discrimination-in-every-other-arena-why-do-we-accept-it-in-religion

DfE (2024) Suspensions and permanent exclusions in England. https://explore-education-statistics.service.gov.uk/find-statistics/suspensions-and-permanent-exclusions-in-england

Education Endowment Foundation (EEF) (2024) *A School's Guide to Implementation: Guidance Report*. https://educationendowmentfoundation.org.uk/education-evidence/guidance-reports/implementation

Etengoff, C. and Lefevor, T.G. (2021) Sexual prejudice, sexism, and religion. *Current Opinion in Psychology, 40*, 45–50. https://psycnet.apa.org/doi/10.1016/j.copsyc.2020.08.024

Gelling, C. (2022) Feminist Views on the Roles of Religions, tutor2u. https://www.tutor2u.net/sociology/reference/sociology-feminist-views-on-the-role-of-religions

Hopster (2019) Is TV Making Your Child Prejudiced? A Report into Pre-School Programming. https://hopster_wordpress_v2.storage.googleapis.com/Hopster-Predjudice-Report-DIGITAL.pdf

Johnson, E. (2015) God Language and Feminist Christology, p1. https://www2.kenyon.edu/Depts/Religion/Projects/Reln91/Gender/godlang&femchristology.htm

NEU (2024) Dress Code, National Education Union. https://neu.org.uk/advice/classroom/dress-code

NEU (2025) Working through the menopause. https://neu.org.uk/advice/equality/sex-and-gender-equality/working-through-menopause

OER (2024) Student diversity: Gender differences in the classroom. https://courses.lumenlearning.com/suny-educationalpsychology/chapter/gender-differences-in-the-classroom

The Key (2023) Whole-school audit: gender and LGBTQ+inclusivity. https://schoolleaders.thekeysupport.com/administration-and-management/ethos-equality/specific-equality-considerations/whole-school-gender-and-lgbtq-inclusivity-audit

Wiltshire Police (2024) Definitions of frequently used words. www.wiltshire.police.uk/police-forces/wiltshire-police/areas/campaigns/campaigns/we-are-listening/definitions-of-frequently-used-words

# 2
# How Can Leaders Develop an Anti-Misogynist Culture in Schools and Classrooms?

## Introduction

This chapter explores how an anti-misogynistic culture starts from the top – from school leaders. It discusses equitable practice for women and girls in schools, and how to develop a strong anti-sexist culture. It delves into how the language we use matters, how it guides practice and how through policy and practice (including behaviour, safeguarding and recruitment), we can support this anti-misogynistic culture. It touches on ideas for raising awareness around issues surrounding violence against women and girls, and how to build links with families and the wider community.

## Leadership, Recruitment and Whole-School Culture

Developing an anti-misogynist culture starts from the top. There must be a commitment from leadership, and it must be threaded throughout all school practices and policies or it will fail. Ask yourself, do your school vision and values align with strong anti-discriminatory practice? If not, it may be time to review your values and vision statement. A really effective way of doing this is involving all stakeholders: staff, pupils, parents, governors. Tell people we are on a journey to develop a culture which is actively anti-misogynistic. Ask people: what words come to mind when you think of our school? Group all the words which are similar – for example, smiles, happiness, joy, and then vote on the word which best represents the word group. You then vote on the words which are the most popular, and you can use these as your values. The school vision should be based on academic culture but also social conduct. Including all stakeholders in this process gives a voice to the community and creates buy-in to the developments you may work on in the future.

## Representation of Women in Leadership

Around the globe, women remain under-represented within school leadership given that nearly seven in ten primary teachers are female (Bergmann et al., 2022), even less so when you take an intersectional approach and look at representation in school leadership through the lens of race and ethnicity coupled with gender. Leaders should be taking responsibility for the culture and infrastructure within their schools, ensuring it is inclusive, starting from policies and procedures including (but not exclusive to) safeguarding, behaviour and wellbeing.

Chamorro-Premuzic (2019) has commented 'so long as we associate leadership with masculine features, we can expect female leaders to be evaluated more negatively even when their performance is higher'. Traditionally, notions of leadership are often connected to perceptions of masculinity, such as being 'strong' and acting with 'gravitas'. In reality, being a successful primary leader is one who is both strong and vulnerable, someone who is driven and compassionate, someone who is commanding and empathetic.

The Department for Education's *School Leadership in England 2010 to 2020: Characteristics and Trends* report (DfE, 2022) documented that on average, women took up their first roles in headship after 19 years in the teaching profession, whereas for men this was 16 years. It found that female teachers were less likely to be promoted to headship or senior leadership than their male counterparts, and furthermore, part-time teachers were 45% less likely than their full-time peers to be promoted. Part-timers were also 51% less likely to be promoted to middle leadership positions.

Who is more likely to be part-time? Women, and more specifically, mums. This is a systemic issue, which requires a commitment to real change from leaders and SLT. Recruitment, selection and promotion processes should be based on competencies which are transparent. This could be experience like collaborative leadership, managing change, analysing data or supporting the development of teaching and learning across the school.

## Representation: What can we do About it?

Here are some suggestions for how we can work to fight this issue.

### Flexible Working

Being committed to flexible working can really help in equitable leadership for women. Flexible working can mean lots of different things, but essentially it's the idea of creating working patterns which suit the employee's needs.

This could be through:

- *Working less than full-time hours*. Part time, job sharing, phased retirement
- *Varied hours*. Staggered hours, compressed hours, annualised hours

- *In-year flexibility*. In lieu time, personal or family days, home or remote working, giving staff the chance to vote for dates of events (e.g. parent's evenings)

Giving time in lieu is a great way to build strong relationships with working parents – allowing time to see performances, sports days, parents' evenings, etc., events that support them with their family life and help when it comes to needing support with events at your school. Two hours given for a morning performance can be two hours helping with your school's summer fair for example.

Women have multiple identities: woman, teacher, leader, mum, partner, wife, carer. It can often feel maddening to merge the different parts of one's identity, which often leads women to feel the solution is choosing just one identity and neglecting the others.

For working mums, flexibility is everything. This should support the development of gender equality in the workplace and allow women to fulfil professional, personal and family commitments guilt free. It should be part of the conversation when supporting women to make career choices after having children.

## Gender Equality vs Gender Parity

Gender equality is about putting systems in place that allow women to be able to achieve professional ambitions whilst fulfilling person and family commitments – making a real difference in their lives. Conversely, gender parity scratches the surface of real change by statically measuring male to female representation in the workforce. While this is useful information to a point, it is only a *part of* the puzzle piece in the journey towards gender equality (Lewis-Lettington, 2021). For example, having an equal number of male and female teachers in a school may show some evidence of gender equality, but what is the *experience* of both? What are their opportunities for leadership? What level of flexibility is given and furthermore encouraged for working mothers, etc.? That's where real gender equality is seen – a staff community where women are enabled to take advantage of leadership development and career growth without having to compromise any other aspects of their lives.

## Equity vs Equality

Inequality in education is complex. Equality is about giving everyone the same resources and opportunities. Conversely, equity recognises that everyone is unique in their lived experiences and the opportunities available to them. It's the understanding that not everyone starts from the same place, and adjustments should be made to make the playing field fairer. Equitable practice means accounting for the different circumstances that people may have, and allocating the appropriate opportunities and resources in order to aim for an equal outcome. Equitable practice understands the impact of intersectional identities on a person's lived experiences and opportunities. School leaders should aim to ensure that practice is equitable for women as it is for men, to be mindful of working parents, staff members' health and other key factors. Having a menopause policy would be an example of equitable practice.

## Menopause Policy

Menopause is a significant time for women, usually occurring between the ages of 45 and 55, defined usually as when a woman's periods have stopped for 12 consecutive months. Menopause can have both positive and negative impacts on a woman's working life. Feminist activist Simone de Beauvoir argued that as women move towards age 50, they develop more wisdom and are set free from the anxiety and mortification of relationships with men. As oestrogen reduces, it changes brain chemistry, making previous insecurities felt by women become less dominant. They become less self-conscious and furthermore less reluctant to challenge and disagree (de Boer and Halsema, 2024).

The National Education Union (NEU, 2025) suggests it is an 'occupational health issue as well as also being an equality issue'. Women should be able to work in a supportive and understanding environment with reasonable adjustments made when going through menopause, have control of the temperature of classrooms and be able to access a toilet when needed (NEU, 2025). Menopause is rarely mentioned in a workplace, particularly when leaders are male. Let's shake things up a bit and do some active work around it as an issue.

## Questions to Consider...

- Do you have a menopause policy and are all staff aware of it? If not, you can find draft templates on The Key or NEU websites
- Is the staff team menopause aware, avoiding women having to raise it as an individual issue?
- How do leaders ensure adequate ventilation in classrooms, staff rooms, etc. to ensure there is good temperature control?
- What systems are in place for cover if a staff member needs to go to the bathroom or get a cold drink mid-teaching?

## Menopause: What can we do About it?

- *Read and learn*. Learn about the menopause and be aware of its impact. A whole workplace approach is needed when supporting those going through menopause. Challenge negative stereotypes and language around the issue to reduce stigma. Symptoms can be hot flushes, heavy or light periods, headaches, urogenital issues, loss of confidence, low mood, poor or reduced concentration, anxiety and panic attacks, joint pain and muscular aches.
- *Adopt a menopause policy*. Use a model example such as the NEU's.
- *View it as a positive*. Supporting staff members experiencing difficulties helps to improve the wellbeing of staff, retains great and experienced teachers, reduces recruitment costs and works towards gender equality.
- *Be flexible*. Offering cover in the short term is better than having to hire new staff members in the long term.

- *Get to know your staff.* Have regular catch-ups so you build trust and are in touch with how they are feeling and what they are experiencing.
- *Give control to female staff over their immediate working environment.* This is empowering.
- *Ensure you have sanitary products available in toilets.* You could have a basket with a variety of different products in your women's toilets.
- *Research and encourage access to support services.* Many local authorities run menopause working groups for employees. Make your whole staff team aware of this and offer cover if there are women who would like to attend the support meetings.
- *Understand that every woman's experience of the menopause is different.* Build a supportive culture at work by having an open-door policy. Find appropriate rooms to talk about it if the staff member wants confidentiality. Follow up and review any actions alongside agreed adjustments.

## Developing Future Female Leaders

Strong appraisal procedures as a leader should work to grow hearts and minds, and spot potential future leaders. As a good leader, you should be able to spot skills in staff members that they may not spot in themselves ... yet.

Being able to recognise future female leaders and support their development is a great step in eliminating misogyny within schools. Furthermore, women leaders can be role models who in turn can normalise the idea and practice of women holding power. The grassroots organisation WomenEd held a campaign called '10% Braver', which aimed to support this kind of work, arguing that with just a little more bravery, women can put themselves out there a little more in order to make progress. Mentoring can be a brilliant way of supporting the development of budding future leaders.

Mentoring can:

- Encourage women to see themselves as potential leaders
- Role model leadership and the journey to get there
- Support women to overcome fear and challenge ideas on their relationship with power
- Support expression without apology – authority looks different depending on the person. It doesn't have to be loud or in your face. Quiet authority can be just as powerful – expression without apology is powerful in itself
- Develop voice – often some women can feel that their voice is not heard. This is particularly the case when viewed through an intersectional lens. Developing a voice, and a way of assertive communication is powerful for leadership development. The ability to be able to confidently express who you are, and use this to your advantage, is vital
- Develop skills in the mentee as well as the mentor! If you have capacity within your team to coach a mentor to in turn coach a mentee, it allows for all parties to grow and develop. Female mentors should be explicit in their own experiences for the benefit of those who follow – deep, honest and open conversations allow for paying it forward

As put by Gorse (2021), 'Every woman who helps another woman to progress makes a change for the better. And this change benefits women everywhere.'

> ### Tip! 2.1
>
> Check out organisations such as WomenEd and Diverse Educators websites for mentoring signposting.

## Words Matter

Core to your school culture are the words and language that are used – how we speak to each other, how we speak to children and how we speak *about* children, matters. Our everyday language through daily interactions, communication with parents and the wider community, and our policies can help to shape an anti-misogynistic culture, one that is intolerant of sexism, sexual harassment and discrimination. Taking a whole-school approach to prevent and address misogyny must sit in the wider infrastructure of the school around safeguarding, behaviour and policies.

Ask yourself, does our language promote mutual respect and model equality for all? Reviewing the words and language used in a school should include looking at:

- Policies
- Procedures
- Letters
- Contracts
- Job descriptions and person specifications

## Policies and Procedures: Behaviour

'It's just banter.' In every school's behaviour policy, there should be explicit reference to sexual harassment and sexism, noting it as a serious incident. That includes the notion of 'banter' – as even the 'low-level' incidents of sexism through jokes and 'banter' can have an extremely damaging effect if left unchallenged. As educators we have a unique position to use our sphere of influence to work towards challenging sexism, using incidents as teachable moments and eliminating prejudice and discrimination against girls and women.

Read your behaviour policy through the lens of tackling sexism, sexual harassment and gender inequality. You may find there are subtle tweaks you can make which will make a far better and more rounded policy.

Check:

- Are sexism and sexual harassment noted as serious incidents?
- Are sexism and sexual harassment noted under the definition of bullying?
- Is there reference to the Equality Act 2010 and that the school is responsible for safeguarding those with a protected characteristic?

- Is there a definition of sexism that includes noting it is both behaviour *and* language?
- Does it note how this will be dealt with if it happens and what consequences there may be?

Staff need to be supported in how to deal with incidents of sexism. Sometimes, accidentally, staff can reinforce gender stereotypes with the language used. Giving staff scripted responses is really useful, as it removes differences in approach between different staff, ensures a consistent response and provides structure and expectation around interactions with children.

There are several different types of responses practitioners can have to misogynistic incidents and behaviour. Jones (2025) describes how a questioning response followed by a confirming response supports using behaviour as teachable moments to increase awareness and reinforce positive anti-discriminatory behaviours.

1. Questioning response:
   - 'What makes you think that?'
   - 'Can you tell me what you mean?'
   - 'Can we talk about why people may think like that?'
2. Confronting response:
   - 'That language is not acceptable.'
   - 'Some people find that offensive and here's why.'

## Seek First to Understand: Teachable Moments

As educators our job is to teach. Often, children use discriminatory language because they may have heard it from another source and/or they may not fully understand the context and gravity of what they say and its impact on others. If we do not teach children this, we have no chance of making real progress.

Reacting emotionally to discriminatory language does not teach the child *why* we do not say and do certain things. Best practice is to use these incidents as teachable moments (whilst of course supporting and protecting any victims too). Getting to the root of where a behaviour comes from helps us understand it and teach appropriate behaviour. Negative behaviour is an opportunity to guide and educate the child to better choices, rather than simply punishing them. Behaviour should be addressed calmly, teachers and leaders should explain why that behaviour is problematic and provide alternative actions to promote positive behaviours and correct what just happened.

## Key Steps

- Seek first to understand the behaviour – why might that child have said/done that? Think about the iceberg model. The behaviour we see is just the tip of the iceberg. Below are all the things going on for that child that might cause this

behaviour, such as neurodiversity, mental health, hunger, pain, stress, frustration, lack of knowledge.
- Ask, 'What happened just before?' to understand the wider context of the behaviour.
- Use a calm and constructive approach, modelling empathy and validating feelings even if the behaviour is unacceptable – for example, 'It is OK to feel frustrated, but it's not OK to exclude people from your game. All feelings are OK, but all behaviours are not.'
- Name the behaviour and describe its impact – for example, 'If we say girls can't play football, that is called misogyny and that is a form of discrimination, just like racism. Discrimination is against the law and against our school rules.'
- Redirect and give advice for the next time the child is in a similar situation – for example, 'Next time you're feeling frustrated at playtime, you could…'.
- Talk about how to rectify the siutation and allow the child to take responsibility for their actions.
- Restorative justice is a strategy to repair wrongdoing and find a positive way forward. Check out restorativejustice.org.uk for more information on this.

---

### Tip! 2.2

Use 'I Time'. Have a laminated sheet with 'I' statements such as:

- I feel…
- I want…
- I am happier when…

When children are discussing a conflict or a behaviour incident, they take it in turns to hold the 'I-Time' sheet and talk through each of the statements, then they swap. At the end, an apology is made and then children can begin to move on, after both speaking and listening to each other. For younger children or children with special educational needs you can use visuals.

---

The benefits of seeking first to understand and teachable moments is that they promote long-term change. They seek to address the underlying reasons for problematic behaviour to make sustainable changes, they can support strengthening relationships and can develop empathy and critical thinking skills. Teaching self-reflection skills from a young age can help to develop these skills to support better behaviour choices in the future.

## Trauma-Informed Practice

All behaviour is communication. Trauma-informed practice supports children suffering with mental health issues or trauma to overcome barriers to learning and school.

When children who have experienced painful life experiences are misunderstood and unsupported, the chances are they will go on to suffer severe mental health difficulties or poor physical health. Schools need a whole-school commitment to trauma-informed practice in order for it to be successful (Trauma Informed Schools UK, 2025).

## Vicarious Trauma

School staff regularly have to deal with stressful situations – Ofsted, challenging pupil behaviour, staff shortages and last-minute cover, school buildings which are not fit for purpose, budget constraints. The list is endless! In addition, leaders have to deal with high-level safeguarding incidents, pupil or parent bereavement, abuse, neglect, victims of serious crime, and have to provide reassurance, comfort and support. Then, at the end of the day, they go home to partners, families or are just by themselves. Leaders often have to suppress their feelings about the barrage of incidents happening at school as their job is to support everyone else.

This is where leaders and school staff can experience vicarious trauma. Vicarious trauma is a reaction to learning about or witnessing the trauma of other people. With vicarious trauma, people can experience a range of profound psychological effects which can stay with them for a long time, particularly if female staff have experienced violence in their own lives too.

It is important that systems of support are put in place to support school staff and leaders, opportunities to talk about psychological effects, inner thoughts, feelings and emotions in a safe space. Staff must be given information about sources of help, and encouraged to reach out and seek free support if needed. This is especially important for leaders, organised by the Headteacher. Headteachers can seek support through their union or other Headteachers.

> ### Tip! 2.3
>
> Regularly share and display wellbeing support in spaces around the school – in the staff room, toilets, etc. The charity Education Support offers free counselling, 24/7. Your local authority or academy trust should also have access to wellbeing support services. In addition, in the case of dealing with a crisis, the local authority may be able to provide clinical supervision through their educational psychology department.

# Policies and Procedures: Safeguarding

Child protection and safeguarding policies must be in line with the most recent guidance. In England this would be *Keeping Children Safe in Education* (DfE 2024), the DfE's statutory guidance document on safeguarding for schools and colleges, and must also be fully understood by all stakeholders in order to keep children safe from all forms of harm. Schools where pupils and families feel there is a genuine commitment to challenging misogyny, sexism, racism and classism, are ones where pupils can start to trust staff enough to open up about abuse.

Understanding contextual safeguarding is imperative in keeping children safe. Developed by Firmin and Lloyd (2020), contextual safeguarding recognises the impact the various environments around children have upon their safety. These include home, family, school, peer group, neighbourhood, and online and physical environments. First we must understand the risks, then we can work towards making them safer. The children in your care will be affected by many factors outside of school. Perhaps there is a local park where there have been incidents of violence against women and girls or there is a poorly lit alleyway which many older children take to get home. Working with families and the local community is imperative in supporting safeguarding. The NSPCC blog written by Meredith (2019) guides educators to keep eyes and ears open for changes in and around the local area such as local public spaces (parks, cafes, bars and shopping areas). Be aware of local sources of support – for example, food banks, support networks or shelters – so that you can help direct families to them when necessary. Also make sure you develop links with statutory agencies in your locality, such as the police and children's services. Create your own database and keep adding to it when you learn about more services – this is an invaluable resource.

> ### Tip! 2.4
>
> Create a safeguarding heat map with children. Print off a school grounds floor map and ask children to colour in the places they find the most and least safe, and discuss why. The least safe places are coloured in red and the most safe in green. This is a key bit of pupil voice relating to safeguarding that can support schools with developing safer spaces.

## Sexual Harassment

Sexism and sexual harassment are rife within our society, and schools are a microcosm of wider society. Acknowledging, and developing practice and policy to eliminate sexual harassment is key for change. One of Ofsted's requirements for schools is to report how exactly they are doing this. Outside of England and Ofsted, there will be other inspectorates who look for similar information also. After leadership, your staff generate the culture at school and must be given proper training and time, encouragement, support and challenges to develop their own behaviours and understanding. This is imperative as they are the people delivering the curriculum. Staff are role models for your pupils. You can have the most anti-misogynistic curriculum but if the people delivering it are not trained properly, it will not be successful. Strong inclusive policies on how *staff* are expected to treat each other should be in place, known, and readily accessible for all – these must include guidance on how to report harassment.

## Sexual Harassment: What Can We do About It?

- *Have a sexual harassment policy.* There are lots of resources on The Key and NEU websites.
- *Provide safe spaces for discussing and reporting harassment.* Are there physical spaces which feel safe for children and staff to speak to someone about something they are worried about? Are there mechanisms for children and staff to ask for help (e.g. worry boxes in classrooms, corridors and leadership offices)? Have you thought about the placement of worry boxes? For example, are they at the front of classrooms and would this prevent a student from posting something? How inclusive are the worry boxes for students with SEND? For example, are there resources (such as symbols, tick boxes and emojis) to enable children with communication difficulties to use a worry box and access asking for help if they cannot read or write? Is there a mechanism for a staff member to ask for help or a private chat – for example, a wellbeing box in the staff room or toilets? Can staff request to meet with a leader via text message if it feels more accessible?
- *Regular opportunities for pupil voice.* What are the mechanisms for pupils to have their voice listened to and how are they adapted to the needs of younger pupils and pupils with additional needs?
- *Set up an equalities committee.* This could be your school council. Give children an opportunity to learn about equity vs equality and speak out on behalf of others.
- *Ensure reporting processes are inclusive* and offer support.
- *Create a bank of local support services.* Signpost additional support.
- *Make sure staff are regularly trained in how to report issues.* This should be in a way that is unbiased and not victim blaming.
- *Communicate with parents.* They should receive clear and regular messages from school that misogyny, sexism and sexual harassment will always be challenged, and make it clear who parents and carers can reach out to if they want to talk.
- *Reconsider school uniform policies.* Some uniform policies disproportionately enforce rules on female clothing.
- *Ensure your team has regular, inclusive training.*
    - Often sexism and homophobia are linked – be sure that your team are well trained on LGBT+ inclusive teaching and that challenging both sexism and homophobia are part of your whole-school approach.
    - Adultification is bias which occurs when children are treated as adults, in terms of their understanding of self, situations and their access to rights. This happens mostly with Black and Brown girls – innocence and vulnerability are not afforded to them. An example in schools is Black and Brown children getting harsher sanctions for the same behaviours as their white peers. Anti-racist practice is closely linked with addressing sexism.
    - Children with a physical difference or who are neurodivergent or LGBT+ are more likely to experience homophobic bullying. Staff must be trained on how the intersection of disability affects sexism and how to approach this (Anti Bullying Alliance, 2015).

- Be mindful of members of marginalised or minority communities, such as the Gypsy Traveller community, in which girls in particular report bullying (58%) more than their male peers (26%) (NEU, 2024).

## White Ribbon Day

Raise awareness about violence against women and girls through events such as White Ribbon Day. White Ribbon is a wonderful charity whose mission is to engage men and boys to end violence against women and girls (VAWG). It aims to prevent men's violence against girls and women by getting to its root causes. The charity works with boys and men to change long-established harmful attitudes, systems and behaviours around rigid gender norms and masculinity which perpetuate violence and inequality. The aim is to stop the violence before it starts.

> ### Tip! 2.5
>
> Each year there is a White Ribbon Day. Use this as a platform to talk about the issue of violence against women and girls and get the community involved. Invite your community, including children, staff and parents, wearing white to show their support. You could run events on the day such as assemblies for children, starting with respect for younger children and moving on to slightly more in-depth conversations about violence with older children. Hold a parent information session, coffee morning, fitness session then chat to raise awareness around VAWG.

As an education setting you can become a 'White Robbin Supporter Organisation' by making seven commitments:

1. Encourage people to wear a White Ribbon and make the White Ribbon Promise to never use, excuse or remain silent about violence against women and girls.
2. Ensure that at least one person in the organisation becomes a White Ribbon Ambassador or Champion.
3. Hold an awareness-raising (and fundraising if appropriate) event each year.
4. Show that you support White Ribbon Day by displaying the Supporter Organisation badge on your website, email signatures and in public places.
5. Mark White Ribbon Day, 25 November, each year.
6. Have policies and guidelines in place that protect staff and support them if they experience harassment, abuse and violence.
7. Ensure people know where they can get help and support by sharing information among staff, through signage and online (White Ribbon, 2025)

## Policies and Procedures: Recruitment

There are several ways to promote gender equality when hiring for school positions. Here are a few key tips:

- *Be sure to use neutral language in job descriptions.* Did you know that statistics show that men will apply for a job where they meet only 60% of the job criteria, whereas women are more likely to apply for a job only if they meet 100% of the criteria? (Leonid, 2025). This means that addressing this head on by labelling job criteria as 'essential' and 'desirable' and being explicit in saying there is some flexibility in candidates meeting the desired criteria may mean more women will apply.
- *Provide flexibility in working hours if possible.* You could offer a full-time role or for four days per week, and you may get a different set of candidates if so. This is more inclusive to working parents too.
- *Train your panel.* Unconscious bias can have a big impact on recruitment. Make sure your interview and shortlisting panel are a diverse group of people and that training is given on unconscious bias and safer recruitment before you start.

---

### Tip! 2.6

Try blind shortlisting. Take out the candidate's name, gender, ethnicity and any equal opportunities forms so that you look at the application alone. The purpose is to reduce bias.

---

## In Summary ...

Culture setting starts from the top, largely set by school leaders. It is the values, behaviours and norms that define the school. Policies and practice underpin the norms and behaviours, which must be in line with the school vision and show a strong, explicit commitment to fight against misogyny and all types of violence against women and girls. Leaders can create a strong anti-misogynistic culture, which empowers female staff to develop and thrive and have opportunities to reach their potential.

## References

Anti Bullying Alliance (2015) Disabled young people that identify as LGBT+bullied and silenced in our schools. https://anti-bullyingalliance.org.uk/aba-our-work/news-opinion/disabled-young-people-identify-lgbt-bullied-and-silenced-our-schools

Bergmann, J., Alban Conto, C. and Brossard, M. (2022) *Increasing Women's Representation in School Leadership: A Promising Path towards Improving Learning.*

Unicef Office of Research. https://inee.org/sites/default/files/resources/Increasing-Womens-Representation-in-School-Leadership-a-promising-path-towards-improving-learning.pdf

Chamorro-Premuzic, T. (2019) As long as we associate leadership with masculinity, women will be overlooked. *Harvard Business Review*, 8 March. https://hbr.org/2019/03/as-long-as-we-associate-leadership-with-masculinity-women-will-be-overlooked

de Boer, M. and Halsema, A. (2024) Mimicking myths of menopause: A critical phenomenological perspective on ageing and femininity in fiction TV shows. *Philosophy & Social Criticism*. https://doi.org/10.1177/01914537241232586

Department for Education (DfE) (2022) *School Leadership in England 2010 to 2020: Characteristics and Trends*. https://assets.publishing.service.gov.uk/government/uploads/system/uploads/attachment_data/file/1071794/School_leadership_in_England_2010_to_2020_characteristics_and_trends_-_report.pdf

Department for Education (DfE) (2024) *Keeping Children Safe in Education 2024*. https://assets.publishing.service.gov.uk/media/66d7301b9084b18b95709f75/Keeping_children_safe_in_education_2024.pdf

Firmin, C. and Lloyd, J. (2020) *Contextual Safeguarding. Her Majesty's Inspectorate of Probation*. www.justiceinspectorates.gov.uk/hmiprobation/wp-content/uploads/sites/5/2020/11/Academic-Insights-Contextual-Safeguarding-CF-Nov-20-for-design.pdf

Gorse, S. (2021) How can we help more women to become school leaders? *TES Magazine*. www.tes.com/magazine/leadership/staff-management/how-can-we-help-more-women-become-school-leaders

Government Equalities Office (2022) *Gender Differences in Response to Requirements in Job Adverts* (https://www.bi.team/wp-content/uploads/2022/03/Gender-differences-in-response-to-requirements-in-job-adverts-March-2022.pdf)

Jones, K. (2025) *Challenging sexism and gender stereotypes in education, Research Hub*. https://my.chartered.college/research-hub/challenging-sexism-and-gender-stereotypes-in-education

Leonid (2025) *5 tips for promoting gender equality when hiring*. www.leonid-group.com/insights/-5-practices-for-promoting-gender-equality-when-hiring

Lewis-Lettington, N. (2021) For working mothers, flexibility is everything. *UN Today*. https://untoday.org/for-working-mothers-flexibility-is-everything

Meredith, C. (2019) *Contextual safeguarding: What is it and why does it matter? NSPCC Learning*. https://learning.nspcc.org.uk/news/2019/october/what-is-contextual-safeguarding

NEU (2024) *Preventing sexism & sexual harassment: Themes and threads*. https://neu.org.uk/advice/equality/sex-and-gender-equality/preventing-sexism-sexual-harassment/preventing-sexism-sexual-harassment-themes-and-threads

NEU (2025) Working through the menopause. https://neu.org.uk/advice/equality/sex-and-gender-equality/working-through-menopause

Trauma Informed Schools & Communities UK (2025) *What is a trauma and mental health informed school or organisation?* www.traumainformedschools.co.uk/home/what-is-a-trauma-informed-school

White Ribbon (2025) *Supporter organisations*. www.whiteribbon.org.uk/supporter-organisations

# 3
# What Does a Feminist Curriculum Look Like?

## Introduction

A feminist curriculum is one which works to disrupt the power dynamics that can often be seen in classrooms, which are microcosms of wider society. This chapter explores what is meant by 'feminism' and what a feminist curriculum looks like; how it is for everyone: men and women, boys and girls and gender nonconforming people. It explores strong anti-sexist practices and representation of women and men across the curriculum, providing a platform to develop teacher subject knowledge and gives auditing tips and tools. It delves into the importance of play in the younger years from an anti-sexist perspective, and how practitioners can create enabling environments ensuring displays, resources and environments are rich, enabling and inclusive.

## Feminism is for all

> 'Feminism is a movement to end sexism, sexist exploitation, and oppression.'
> (bell hooks, 2000)

The term 'patriarchy' simply means institutionalised sexism. This sexism is one which affects both women *and* men – the sooner we realise this the sooner we can start to unravel it. The way that we unravel it is through feminism. The label 'feminist' has often been linked with being inherently man-hating but this is not what feminism is about. Feminism isn't about hating men. Feminism is about a commitment to equality. All people, irrespective of gender, sexuality, race or disability, should be treated with respect and dignity – feminism is inclusive and is about dismantling systems of oppression in order for women, men and gender nonconforming people to hold equal rights, resources and power.

The patriarchy harms men and boys by pressuring them to conform to ideals of aggressive masculinity, and in many cases leaves them feeling isolated when they do not express their emotions or ask for help. Qualities like this do not align with the patriarchal view of what it means to be a man.

Feminism is for all, including children, as it is the belief that everyone is equal, irrespective of gender. It is about crafting a more equal world and teaching that when we are all equal, all of us are more free. Through a carefully planned curriculum, educators can use their sphere of influence to challenge harmful stereotypes, promote equality and self-care and develop advocacy and strong allyship in children.

## A Note on Feminist Pedagogy

Feminist pedagogy is understood as one where classrooms are built on co-construction of knowledge and skills, facilitating connections between students and teachers, as opposed to a teacher simply telling students information. The classroom is seen as a space of community and sets to disrupt some of the power dynamics that can underpin some classrooms. The idea behind this pedagogy started with the understanding that hierarchies and institutions dominated by men were built on educational systems which disempowered women and girls, hindering their opportunities for true success. Furthermore, intersectional feminist pedagogies acknowledge the ways that race, disability, ethnicity, class, age, gender identity, and sexuality further compound inequality, often creating barriers to learning (University of Notre Dame, 2024).

## Challenging Stereotypes Through Representation

Representation matters – children cannot be what they cannot see. Inclusive schools work hard to ensure children can see both themselves represented through the curriculum, but also be exposed to a range of depictions of women showing different experiences and dispelling stereotypes in doing so.

### Representation Through Text

Representation within literature is extremely important when engaging young learners in reading. When children are able to see themselves, in some way or another, they are more invested and interested in stories. This is especially the case for children from disadvantaged backgrounds, and those whose intersectional positionings may place them at a disadvantage or lead to discrimination. It goes beyond simply having books with female leads. It's deeper than that. It is about drilling down into the true representation of gendered character traits and ensuring they are not reinforcing gender stereotypes, and in doing so there are four basic types of gender stereotyping:

1. *Personality traits*. Women are emotional and nurturing, whilst men are strong, confident and aggressive.
2. *Domestic behaviours*. Women cook, clean and take care of children whilst men do home repairs, look after finances, fix the car, etc.
3. *Occupations*. Women work in nurturing or giving roles such as nursing and teaching, whilst men take jobs in protection or action roles as police officers, pilots, doctors and engineers.

4   *Physical appearance.* Women are thin, graceful with no body hair and whilst men are muscular and tall.

When children see characters with their gender consistently showing up in their books, it may cause them to conform to and perpetuate the stereotypical behaviour and traits they see. Children's books, even now, feature males more frequently than females and furthermore, non-human characters (such as animals) are more likely to be male than female. For example, characters like bears, lions and dragons are more likely to be male, reinforcing the strong, hyper-masculine character, whereas females are more likely to be smaller, more delicate animals such as birds. These not only reinforce self-perceptions meaning that children are more likely to conform to harmful gender stereotypes, but they can also limit their capacity to be open minded and think critically.

We really need to actively resist texts with these stereotypes so as to provide children with a platform to start thinking critically about gender stereotypes and be inspired to do whatever makes their heart sing. This is an act of feminism.

## Tip! 3.1

- Audit the representation of gender in your library or book corner. Pick six books at random and look into the representation of male and female characters. You can also consider the authors of books and ensure you have books written by women, men and gender nonconforming people, from a range of intersectional identities. This will help you understand your current offer, and begin to think about how to change it.
- Appeal to the wider community for help. Why not create an Amazon wishlist full of books which challenge gender stereotypes, explain to the school community what you are doing and why, and send out the wishlist to your parent community and beyond? You'll end up with heaps of books and your budget doesn't have to take the hit.
- Once you buy new texts, keep a record of which classrooms contain which books so you have a clear understanding of how you are meeting the needs of the children. Literacy leads! If you were to keep this on a whole-school database, you would then be able to track the development of text throughout the school.
- Provide children with a reading list and incentivise them with a prize if they read a certain number of books. Give them the titles of the books and non-gendered descriptions, such as 'This book is about a child who goes on a frightening adventure.' Where authors have not specified the gender of a character – for example, a non-human character – vary the gender pronoun that you use rather than reverting to 'he/him' each time.
- Diversify the book offer and put a spotlight on particular books which challenge gender stereotypes to generate interest.
- Pick an 'Author of the week' and display three or four books from that author, amplifying female voices and characters challenging gender norms.

Here is a list of books which actively challenge gender stereotypes and are a good place to start:

3-5 year olds:

- *Rosa Plays Ball* by Jessica Spanyol
- *Pink is for Boys* by Eda Kaban and Robb Pearlman
- *Mary Wears What She Wants* by Keith Negley
- *Julián is a Mermaid* by Jessica Love

6-8 year olds:

- *Look Up!* by Dapo Adeola and Nathan Bryan
- *Large Fears* by Myles E. Johnson
- *The Boy & The Bindi* by Vivek Shraya and Rajni Perera
- *The Night Pirates* by Peter Harris and Deborah Allwright
- *10,000 Dresses* by Marcus Ewert and Rex Ray

9-11 year olds:

- *Ada Twist, Scientist* by Andrea Beaty and David Roberts
- *Stories for Boys Who Dare to Be Different* by Ben Brooks
- *Women in Sports* by Rachel Ignotofsky
- *Gender Swapper Fairytales* by Karrie Fransman and Jonathan Plackett
- *Queer Heroes* by Arabelle Sicardi and Sarah Tanat-Jones
- *What is Gender? How Does It Define Us? And Other Big Questions for Kids* by Juno Dawson

Books are powerful. They are a medium to inspire, empower and communicate with children. They are a gateway for children to understand themselves, others and the world around them. Developing strong representation through text helps children to develop empathy for others, think critically about the world around them, and to be creative and open-minded.

## Birth to 5: Play as a Tool for Dismantling Gender Stereotypes

Play matters. It is a vital part of child development and can shape lifelong attitudes and ambitions. This is why the early years are arguably the most formative and important parts of a child's school journey. Children need a wide range of activities to develop a wide range of skills. Toys and the stereotypes they communicate limit children's choices, affecting their self-esteem and self-image, and limiting their expectations. When we signpost gendered toys – either explicitly or sometimes accidentally – we affect a child's experience of play and development of self, limiting possible interests. Challenging stereotypes in the early years is now part of both Ofsted's good and outstanding grade descriptors, which is a positive move. This created a seismic shift in many early years settings and a platform for children to enjoy and learn from creative play without boundaries.

Most EYFS practitioners recognise and want to eliminate harm caused by gender stereotypes. However, many practitioners unintentionally separate girls and boys. This can be done inadvertently through language or physical segregation, and children's interests can be influenced towards stereotypical behaviour.

EYFS practitioners should do the following:

- Offer play options that actively challenge gender stereotypes by encouraging children to engage with a range of different activities.
- Encourage children to explore activities which counter gender stereotypes, such as boys engaging in nurturing and caring games and girls engaging in risk-taking play.
- Affirm unconventional choices and reassure children that it's OK to be different. This helps to encourage a culture of acceptance. For example, a parent may question boys dressing up as Disney princesses – the role of the practitioner is to support the children's choices.
- Have opportunities to reflect on their own unconscious biases and what impact these may have on their practice. Knowing helps us to change and develop (Henderson, 2022).
- Challenge stereotypes when they arise. For example, if a child says, 'Boys don't wear pink', you could respond with 'That's funny, my dad wears pink'.
- Analyse spaces by how they are used and who is using them. Are there certain areas dominated by particular groups of children, or by one gender? Think about changes you could make to encourage all children to feel equally free to use the reading corner, the home corner, the bikes, the Lego, the outdoor space, etc. Consider colour coding, signage and/or staffing.
- Use gender neutral language and do not divide the class by gender. Rather than referring to groups of children as 'girls' or 'boys' you could say 'children' or 'everyone'.

> **Tip! 3.2**
>
> Strong early years leadership should actively challenge gender stereotypes as a priority – it's about changing the whole ecosystem of EYFS practice. Ensure this is in action plans and is shared with the whole team, so everyone is moving in the same direction. Complete regular reviews of gender and intersecting stereotypes, and include the whole team in examining resources, materials and outcomes. This way you can get buy-in from the whole team and allow all practitioners to have a voice in school development.

## Case Study: Iceland

Iceland is high in the rankings of the best places in the world to live as a woman. It was the first country to make it illegal to pay women less than men for the same job and new parents get a whole year of parental leave. At a nursery in Reykjavik, girls are encouraged to be unapologetic and fearless (with activities like log throwing) whereas boys are encouraged to be gentle and nurturing with activities such as hair brushing and creative dance. The idea is to allow children to develop without the constraints of gender stereotyping. Violence against women and girls here is still prevalent (BBC, 2024). Iceland is an interesting contradiction, as despite the advances in gender equality, there has been a surge of domestic violence reports by nearly 40% in the last

10 years (Bertini et al, 2025). This indicates that the violence is happening, but also that women are empowered to report it – comparative figures from the UK show a gradual decrease in reported domestic abuse but an increase in sexual assault (Office for National Statistics, 2024). This raises questions about the number of reported incidents vs the actual picture for women, and what other societal factors are at play which feed into this. For example, if the UK worked to eliminate the gender pay gap as Iceland has begun to done, would women feel more empowered to report intimate partner violence when it happens, resulting in a surge of domestic violence reports? Or is the surge in Iceland due to more violence?

I wonder how the UK can learn from this system.

## Representation of Women Throughout the Curriculum

Take stock of the representation of women across the taught units in your curriculum, ensuring that there are topics which explore and challenge gender stereotypes as well as opportunities to explore intersectional identities too. If you are teaching about women's suffrage, ensure that you study the lives of the Black suffragette Sarah Parker Remond and Indian suffragettes Sophia Duleep Singh and Lolita Roy, for example.

## Use Modelled Writing to Build Empathy

The perspective from which we write matters. If we always write from the perspective of a white heterosexual male from a nuclear family, we don't give children opportunities to put themselves in someone else's shoes, to think from different perspectives from their own. This must be modelled by teachers and named whilst doing it.

> ### Tip! 3.3
>
> As you are modelling, you can think aloud saying things like, 'I wonder what it must feel like to be this character …' or 'this character is different from me, let me think hard about how they must feel …'

When planning a writing sequence, be sure to think carefully about the protagonists in your narratives. For example, do you have equal numbers of stories written from a female and male character's perspective? Have you written a story from the perspective of a person with a disability? Does the main voice of the story/writing have a 'nuclear family' or something different? You could note on your long-term plan at the start of the year the perspective from which each session of modelled writing is written, so you can keep track of the range of voices.

These learning experiences facilitate building empathy with others whilst also providing visibility for marginalised children. This is a great opportunity for building diversity and inclusion!

## Representation in History

'So when you study history, you must ask yourself, Whose story am I missing? Whose voice was suppressed so that this voice could come forth? Once you have figured that out, you must find that story too.' (Gyasi, 2016)

History is the stories told by those who held power – women's history has historically been overlooked. As practitioners, we must be sure to actively include women's stories – not just the women who achieved success and high status, but also the women who remain largely unnamed in history, and those who have quietly shaped our way of life today.

Here are some significant individuals who could be added or weaved into the key stage 1 primary history curriculum:

*Noor Inayat Khan – secret agent*. Noor was a wartime British secret agent of Indian descent. She was the first female radio operator to be sent into Nazi-occupied France by the Special Operations Executive.
*Elizabeth Fry – social activist*. Known for helping those in need, she was a deeply religious woman who is particularly known for her work in prisons. She fervently believed that all people, including prisoners, should be treated with kindness and respect. There's some useful information on her on the BBC Bitesize website.
*Mary Anne Galton – social activist*. In 1806, Mary Anne Galton moved to Bristol and was one of many women who protested against the slave trade by abstaining from buying and eating sugar. This fight was led by women who ran households, taking the lead on abstaining from sugar.
*Rosa May Billinghurst – suffragette*. A wheelchair user, she attended all her rallies in her wheelchair, and even chained herself to the railings at Buckingham Palace.
*Mary Seacole* – nurse. Mary was a British Jamaican nurse and businesswoman who cared for soldiers during the Crimean War whilst overcoming injustice and racism.
*Grace O'Malley – Pirate Queen of Ireland*. A fierce leader, she defended the independence of her territory at a time when large parts of Ireland were coming under British rule.
*Wangarĩ Maathai – political activist*. The founder of the Green Belt Movement, a movement which empowered women through the planting of trees. She was a Kenyan social, environmental and political activist who fought for women's rights.

Here are some women to explore when looking at the role of women in ancient civilisations, such as the Egyptians, at key stage 2:

*Nefertiti – Egyptian queen*. Reigning as queen of Egypt from 1353 to 1336 BC, alongside the pharaoh Akhenatem, she was a powerful woman and seen as a living goddess.
*Cleopatra – queen of Egypt*. Cleopatra VII Thea Philopator ruled Egypt before it was taken over by the Roman Empire. She was actually Greek and not Egyptian at all. She was born around 69 BC and ruled for around 21 years in the Egyptian city of Alexandria. She was regarded as highly intelligent – she would often read scrolls from the library of Alexandria – and she spoke both ancient Egyptian and Greek.

There are many historians who believe she brought peace to Egypt during one of its most challenging times.

When learning about the Shang Dynasty, you could include:

*Fu Hao – high priestess and military general.* Fu Hao was the army leader and powerful ruler who had up to 13,000 troops and won many battles. In 1976, her grave was excavated, proving to be a deeply significant find containing a vast number of artefacts and precious items, which have informed historians on life in the Shang Dynasty. This provides children with a great opportunity to develop historical skills in understanding and interpreting evidence. Show children photos of the artefacts found in her tomb and ask, 'How can we use these artefacts to learn about Shang times?'

When learning about the Romans, you could include:

*Female gladiators.* Historians have found some evidence in written accounts and arts that women of all classes also participated as gladiators. There is evidence that women sparred with each other and fought beasts in spectacles ordered by emperors Nero, Titus and Domitian. Some women were encouraged to get involved as it was believed it could build strength for childbirth (Beck, 2022). Ask children, 'What does a gladiator look like?' Then use this as a way into discussing and challenging gender stereotypes.

## Thematic History: Themes Through Time

In key stage 2, pupils are expected to undertake a chronological study of a period of history beyond 1066. This could be a significant turning point in history post 1066 or it could be a study of a theme over a long period of time, such as leisure, technology, medicine or crime and punishment. You could use the theme of social justice fighters for this and study different campaigns for equality, delving into similarities. Here are some examples:

- *The Stonewall Riots 1969.* A key individual was Marsha P. Johnson, LGBT+ and trans activist
- *Fight for race equality.* Key individuals included Claudia Jones, an anti-racist activist and a founding spirit of the Notting Hill Carnival
- *UK Black Pride.* Taking an intersectional look at equality, Phyll Opoku-Gyimah, otherwise known as Lady Phyll, is a British LGBT+ rights activist and anti-racism campaigner

Key women in non-European society studied in key stage 2 could include:

*Zubayda bint Ja'far al-Mansur.* Zubayda was from Baghdad and was mainly famous for making the pilgrimage to Mecca safer by funding way-stations and wells between Baghdad and Mecca in the 8th and 9th century. She was said to be the most powerful and the richest woman in the world and is remembered for the reservoirs and artificial pools and wells which were also built on this path. Ask children, 'What do you think it was like to go on a Haj during the time Zubayda lived? What might the Haj be like if she hadn't done the work she did?

*Lady K'abel – Mayan 'supreme warrior'.* Lady K'abel was a Mayan military ruler and queen. As the warrior queen, her role was more important than the King's. Similar to Fu Hao, when her tomb was found in 2012 in Guatemala, she was found with lots of artefacts which taught historians much about the 7th Century Maya. Maya hieroglyphs on the back of an alabaster jar found in her tomb included the names 'Lady Water Lily Hand' and 'Lady Snake Lord'.

## Representation of Women in Science

Did you know that the first computer algorithm, the discovery of new elements, forces and other building blocks of nature and stellar classification systems were all fundamental discoveries made by women?

Women have been historically under-represented in science and still make up the minority of careers in STEM subjects (science, technology, engineering and mathematics). In science it is important to challenge gender stereotypes and use counter-stereotypical images, career slides, and stories and literature that show women's contributions to science. Negative stereotypes around girls' participation in STEM subjects in early years can result in a lifelong impact on women's career choices, causing a gender digital divide and large-scale economic impact (Unicef, n.d.).

> ### Tip! 3.4
> The Perimeter Institute does a free set of beautiful posters called 'Forces of Nature' about women scientist role models – great for displaying around the school!

Here are some key female scientists you could add into your science curriculum.

*Dr Claudia Alexander.* A fierce advocate for both women and other minorities in science. She was an expert in planetary science and geophysics and worked as a scientist for NASA (O'Flynn, 2017).

*Vera Rubin.* An astronomer who advocated for women in science, she discovered that galaxies have flat rotation curves and contributed greatly to physics theory (O'Flynn, 2017).

*Vivienne Malone-Mayes.* She was one of the first African American women to achieve a PhD in mathematics. She also participated in the civil rights movement, fighting persistent racism and sexism in her career (O'Flynn, 2017).

Maths4Girls is a great initiative provided for free by Founders4Schools, an ed-tech charity, which helps teachers increase the number of girls pursuing maths beyond

GCSE level. It has created a platform of current role models in the field of maths and connects girls with professional women in maths careers. It has resources to support role model events and lots of tips – it's a great resource to tap into.

## Representation of Men Throughout the Curriculum

Historically, men have dominated many documented fields and this is reflected in who and what is taught across primary curriculum subjects. Even where schools do make efforts to include notable women in given fields, as a whole, men (predominantly white men) still dominate and this sends powerful messages to children.

When we think about representation of men in the primary curriculum, we are not thinking about adding more, we are thinking about the *quality* and *range* of different male experiences represented to ensure that we are not reinforcing potentially harmful stereotypes about boys and men.

We need to provide a range of representation of men showing children real-life examples that counter stereotypes, male role models in nurturing careers as well as inventors and explorers, male experiences showing stereotypically 'female traits' such as empathy and emotional literacy, sensitivity, warmth and gentleness, helpfulness and understanding, sweetness and modesty, emotional capacity, kindness and affection. This representation creates a safe space for boys to be able to explore the range of human emotions and experiences and not be pigeonholed as 'man=strong'.

## Representation of Trans and Gender Nonconforming People

Gender nonconforming people have always existed since the beginning of time (although some right-wing tabloids may try to convince people otherwise). We are on a journey to better knowledge and there is improved visibility for trans and gender nonconforming people. The issue isn't that they are new, but that governments have failed to recognise them. It is important that there is strong representation in the curriculum of gender nonconforming people and trans people in the curriculum and that schools are made welcoming places for people who identify as either (or both).

Studies have found that gender nonconforming people make up nearly 11% of all LGBTQ+people. Despite this, the recognition of gender nonconforming people throughout history and their rights has been slow-moving worldwide (GenderGP, 2024).

In countries such as Nepal, Uruguay, Argentina, Iceland and Australia non-binary identities are legally recognised. In other countries such as India and Pakistan, genders like the kinnar (an Urdu word for transgender) and *khawaja sira* (third gender – neither male or female) are recognised. However, in many countries (like the UK), non-binary people can't yet have their correct gender marker on their legal documents or IDs (GenderGP, 2024) as it is thought by the UK government to be 'too complex' to introduce, despite sex and gender reassignment being a protected characteristic in the 2010 Equality Act.

## A Note on Terms

- *Transgender* 'is a broad term that can be used to describe people whose gender identity is different from the gender they were thought to be when they were born. "Trans" is often used as shorthand for transgender' (Advocates for Trans Equality, n.d.).
- *Gender nonconforming* is defined as 'not adhering to society's gender norms. People may describe themselves as gender nonconforming if they don't conform to the gender expression, presentation, behaviors, roles, or expectations that society sees as the norm for their gender. People of any gender identity can be gender nonconforming' (Fournier, 2024). Someone can be both transgender *and* gender nonconforming, but not all transgender people are gender nonconforming.
- *Two-spirit* is an umbrella term that some First Nations and Native American people use to 'describe identities that exist beyond male and female. They do not correspond to non-Native structures of gender. In Hawaii, māhū are non-binary people with a rich history of important spiritual and social roles' (GenderGP, 2024).

---

**Tip! 3.5**

Add your pronouns onto your work email signature and your staff badges. This brings attention to the importance of respecting people's identities and creates space for gender nonconforming people who use neither masculine nor feminine pronouns to be open about how they identify.

---

## Gender Nonconforming in History

In Roman Britain, Cataractonium, which is present-day Catterick in North Yorkshire, is one of the first LGBT locations found. There, archaeologists uncovered a 4th century grave of a 'gallus'. Born as a man, a gallus became a priestess of goddess Cybele by self-castrating, cross-dressing and taking on a woman's role to demonstrate their commitment to Cybele. Jet jewellery and other 'female' accessories were found in the grave. The discovery of their social and cultural role highlights the gender diversity that existed in Roman Britain (Historic England, n.d.).

In the Byzantine Empire, some females went on to join all-male orders of monks, using both female and male pronouns interchangeably.

French warrior Joan of Arc, famous for leading the French army to victory over the English in the Hundred Years' War, used female pronouns. Despite this, when she was called by God, she took up exclusively masculine clothing and social roles (GenderGP, 2024).

## Strong PSHE

It goes without saying that teaching strong PSHE (Personal, Social, Health and Economic Education) is a brilliant way to teach, discuss and challenge children on a range of issues surrounding keeping themselves safe and building meaningful relationships with others around them. Gendered stereotype narratives can put women and girls at risk by promoting unhealthy relationship behaviours and victim blaming which can normalise sexual harassment and abuse (PSHE Association, 2023).

Toxic gendered stereotypes are deeply damaging to children's self-image and self-esteem, and affect how they treat others around them – from deep insecurities about body image and agency to normalising abusive behaviours. PSHE is vital in safeguarding children and building understanding and resistance to problematic narratives.

The world around us is full of messages on how we 'should' be or act. Unrealistic beauty norms cause children – from a young age – to have low self-esteem, issues with body confidence and poor mental health. The unyielding pressure to be perfect can impact children's perceptions of self, leading to confidence issues, mental health issues and in some cases, self-harm. Harbouring an unrealistic body image can lead to unhealthy eating habits and disorders among both girls and boys.

Strong PSHE should teach the idea of consent – giving permission *freely* and accepting no as a valid response from the early years. Teachers should model asking for consent, encouraging others to ask, and teaching children to accept others saying no.

---

**Tip! 3.6**

Many primary children love to hug adults around school. If this happens to you, model stepping back and prompting 'please ask for consent'. When children ask, you can sometimes say yes, but also sometimes say no. This creates space for children to do this with each other too.

---

## Developing Oracy: Conversation Not Debate

The main difference between a conversation and a debate is that a conversation aims to understand, whereas a debate aims to *win*. When we are teaching children and challenging stereotypes, we must engage in conversation not debate. Conversations allow for listening to each other and building trust and empathy.

Developing great oracy in classrooms is imperative as it supports children to develop communication, problem solving and reasoning skills, which are essential for both academic success but also for developing meaningful relationships and keeping themselves safe.

### Amplifying Girl's Voices

It is an unfortunate fact that women and girl's voices around the world are often not heard. As mentioned at the start of this chapter, our classrooms are microcosms of wider society – who is heard and who is not define the status quo. In many classrooms, boys are the dominant voice. Theirs are the voices that dominate conversations, and they are the most confident to share ideas. As teachers, we must proactively work to amplify girls' voices in the classroom. Research has found that teachers are more likely to interrupt girls than boys, that they spend more time prompting boys to seek deeper answers than they do girls and praise boys' contributions whereas they praise girls for being quiet (Barron, 2024).

Voice 21, a national charity that supports the development of oracy in children, suggests three tips for amplifying girls' voices within the classroom.

1. *Get expectations right.* Expectations for classroom talk must be set high. It has to be the expectation that everyone will contribute in some way. Set talk guidelines for the children in your classroom, display them and expect children to follow them. Behaviours include not interrupting each other, active listening, how to respond to others and non-verbal communication. The ground rules are extremely important.
2. *Value everyone's voices.* Girls must be actively encouraged to become pupil leaders, school councillors, prefects etc. Having strong female role models in leadership positions will empower other girls around the school to feel more confident in using their voices.
3. *Teach oracy.* Be sure to talk about talk with children, giving them chances to reflect on the talk that is happening. Voice 21 encourages teachers to teach girls, specifically, how to talk and make sure that people are listening. This could be through teaching how to challenge or clarify with sentence stems such as 'I'd like to challenge you on that' or 'I'm not sure you understood what I was saying – what I meant was …' or 'I'm not finished speaking, you can share your idea next'. Teachers can model these expectations, sentence stems and ways of speaking to ensure it is fully embedded (Barron, 2024).

### Tip! 3.7

Why not create chances in assemblies for children to have discussions about key topics. These are *conversations*, not debates. Each week you could have an expert panel of children who feel passionate about the topic such as 'TikTok has changed the world – but for better or worse?' or 'Gaming makes children smarter.'

## Enabling Environments: Displays, Resources

Enabling environments are just that – spaces where children are enabled to feel safe and included and seen. What do the displays and corridors show? Are there displays challenging gender stereotypes, showing role models in different aspects of school life, careers and beyond?

Here are some ways teachers can create stimulating environments, which are accessible to all:

- *Books, books, books!* Review your book corners and/or school libraries to ensure there is strong representation of texts which challenge gender stereotypes and amplify female voices. Ensure an intersectional approach. Try having a 'Book of the week' or 'Author of the month' working display in your room.
- *Celebrate diversity and intersectional identities.* Try to include photos and biographies of role models on your displays.
- *Consider gender-neutral bathrooms.* This makes sure all children can comfortably and safely use the bathroom without having to use a toilet which doesn't match their gender identity. Even if you can facilitate having one block of gender-neutral toilets, this is better than none. It is also important to still provide single-sex toilets in addition, so that there are safe spaces for children to go to the toilet and that school is in line with school guidance.
- *Encourage emotional expression.* Ensure every classroom and office (e.g. the headteacher's office) has a worry box for children to be able to express concerns without fear of judgement or consequences – see page 27 for more information on this. By allowing space to articulate their worries, children develop emotional awareness. They can learn to identify and manage their feelings more effectively. Think about how to make these accessible to all. If you have a number of children who would struggle writing how they feel you could have an emoji sheet where they tick or circle the emotion/s they are feeling.
- *Normalise speaking about emotions.* Start each day or each session by asking children how they feel. You could do this by simply asking them, or showing a range of different expressions and asking them to pick, or even teach children the Makaton symbols for different emotions. When children respond, encourage them to look around the room and notice how others are feeling too, so it's not simply an exchange between the teacher and the child, it builds empathy between peers too.

---

**Tip! 3.8**

Class names are a really easy way to build in representation. Why not name your classes after people who defy gender stereotypes? A good way to build pupil voice into this is to provide children with two options at the start of the year – share the key information about each person and then ask children to vote for which person they would like to be their class name. You can then get children to do research, art or a piece of writing and you have a year-long, informative display!

---

## Auditing

To know where you are going, you need to know where you are now. This is done through auditing. Auditing is very much a team effort – it is not solo work! If you are going to do work on developing a feminist curriculum and anti-sexist practice, this work needs to be part of the school's strategic plan with aligned professional development to support learning and teaching. A gender audit will let you evaluate the current status and range of resources and experiences available across the school.

The aim of auditing is to think about:

- Strengths in the curriculum offer
- Weaknesses or gaps in the curriculum offer
- How CPD supports teaching
- How resources support learning and development

Auditing is a process which takes significant time if it is going to be meaningful. It is the gathering of evidence from a range of sources in order to draw conclusions about the above list. It cannot be completed in one staff meeting, and teachers must be given time out of class in order to have the headspace to do it justice.

Diversity of thought is important when auditing – a homogenous group of people will have the same knowledge gaps. Who you invite to the table matters. Consider how you can put together a diverse group of auditors: teachers with different amounts of teaching experience, male and female, leaders and non-leaders, teachers and non-teachers, different ethnicities, abilities and lived experiences. You may wish to set up working groups for different areas – for example, a group to amplify girls' voices and another to look at the representation of women in history.

## What to Look at When Auditing?

- Curriculum maps and long-, medium- and short-term plans
- A small sample of lesson plans (just to get a feel of practice – you absolutely don't need to be studying *every* individual lesson plan!)
- Pupil book study – looking at pupil books *with* children and having discussions about learning. You'll also be able to see which learning has stuck with them and which hasn't and then consider why
- Trips, workshops and first-hand experiences such as special events
- Assemblies/collective worship
- Policies – teaching and learning, individual subjects, anti-bullying, behaviour and wellbeing, child protection, online safety, etc.
- Displays – do they show images of women, men and gender nonconforming people and actively confront gendered stereotypes?
- School website

### Tip! 3.9

Don't reinvent the wheel with a bespoke audit. There are many great gender audits available for you to use, a great one being on The Key. Your local authority/diocese/academy trust might already have one you can use and you could team up with a local school to audit each other's offer to include even more voices.

## In Summary ...

A feminist curriculum is for all – this is not a women's issue, it's an everyone issue! Children cannot be what they cannot see. A feminist curriculum is rooted in strong representation across the curriculum – for girls, boys and gender nonconforming people. Representation which shows the scope of humanity redefines strength and vulnerability, promotes healthy masculinity and empowers girls to use their voices and have them amplified. Representation matters because it allows children to experience diverse perspectives and fosters a deep sense of empathy and belonging whilst combating harmful stereotypes and promoting inclusivity.

## References

Advocates for Trans Equality (n.d.) Understanding transgender people: The basics. https://transequality.org/issues/resources/understanding-transgender-people-the-basics

Barron, G. (2024) Amplifying girls' voices in the classroom and beyond. Voice 21 https://voice21.org/amplifying-girls-voices-in-the-classroom-and-beyond

BBC (2024) Iceland has dominated the rankings as the best place for women to live for nearly two decades. Instagram, 7 December. www.instagram.com/bbcnews/reel/DDSMRRnowOz

Beck, M. (2022) Did women fight as gladiators in Ancient Rome? History, A&E Television Networks. https://groups.io/g/ForAllThings/topic/did_women_fight_as_gladiators/90038828

Bertini, R., Pompei, E., Briend-Guy, J. and Raud, M. (2025) Iceland's dark shadow: gender-based violence in a model nation, France 24. Available at: https://www.france24.com/en/europe/20250308-iceland-dark-shadow-gender-based-violence-in-a-model-nation-women

Fournier, A. (2024) What does gender nonconforming mean? www.verywellmind.com/gender-nonconforming-definition-4582878

GenderGP (2024) Non-binary people in history and across cultures. www.gendergp.com/non-binary-people-in-history

Gyasi, Y. (2016) *Homegoing*. Penguin Random House.

Henderson, A. (2022) Small but mighty steps to tackle gender stereotypes. Fawcett Society. www.fawcettsociety.org.uk/blog/small-but-mighty-steps-to-tackle-gender-stereotypes

Historic England (n.d.) Trans and gender-nonconforming histories. https://historicengland.org.uk/research/inclusive-heritage/lgbtq-heritage-project/trans-and-gender-nonconforming-histories

hooks, b. (2000) *Feminism Is for Everybody: Passionate Politics*. Pluto Press.

O'Flynn, E. (2017) Forces of nature: Great women who changed science. Perimeter Institute. https://perimeterinstitute.ca/news/forces-of-nature-great-women-who-changed-science

Office for National Statistics (2024) Crime in England and Wales: year ending December 2024. Available at: https://www.ons.gov.uk/peoplepopulationandcommunity/crimeandjustice/bulletins/crimeinenglandandwales/yearendingdecember2024#:~:text=Experiences%20of%20domestic%20abuse%2C%20sexual,people)%20had%20experienced%20sexual%20assault

PSHE Association (2023) Misogyny, online influencers and the PSHE curriculum. https://pshe-association.org.uk/guidance/ks1-5/misogyny-online-influencers-and-the-pshe-curriculum

Unicef (n.d.) Dismantling stereotypes to drive equality. www.unicef.org/media/117536/file/Dismantling%20stereotypes%20in%20media%20and%20advertising%20to%20drive%20equality_UNICEF%202022.pdf

University of Notre Dame (2024) Incorporating feminist pedagogy into your courses. https://learning.nd.edu/resource-library/incorporating-feminist-pedagogy-into-your-courses

World Bank Group (n.d.) Gender Data Portal. Iceland. https://genderdata.worldbank.org/en/economies/iceland

# 4
# Positive Masculinities

## Introduction

This chapter explores the idea of empowering young men and boys to cultivate healthy, respectful and positive expressions of masculinity, looking at various topics and activities that will help teachers support boys to develop self-awareness, build healthy relationships and navigate societal expectations with confidence. Positive masculinity is about allowing space for boys to be their authentic selves and embracing empathy, kindness and respect for all. This is to counteract the idea of 'toxic masculinity' and incorporate pupil voice.

> 'The biggest lie is that the fight to address male suffering is separate or at odds with the battle to liberate women. We all experience gender. We are all limited by oppressive gender stereotypes.' (Liz Plank, 2019, p. 34)

## Moving Away from the Notion of Toxic Masculinity

The notion of masculinity is not a fixed male identity but multiple, complex and intersectional social attitudes, behaviours and experiences which are both fluid and often contradictory. Whilst masculinity itself is not inherently toxic, toxic masculinity is everywhere. It's in the books we read, the programmes we watch, the adverts we see, the social media we scroll through. Boys are constantly confronted by a toxic representation of what it means to be a man. The term toxic masculinity refers to the set of behaviours and attitudes stereotypically associated with men, and is thought to have a negative impact on boys, men and society as a whole. It is full of destructive messages leading men to feel inadequate and entitled, perpetuates dominance and ultimately leads to engagement in misogyny, homophobia and violence against women and girls. In addition, the biggest killer in men under 40 years old is suicide.

Toxic masculinity has four main facets:

1 Men should be *tough*, physically strong, tough and aggressive.
2 Men should *not be feminine*, should not show emotions or accept help.
3 Men should be *powerful* and hold dominance in social and financial systems.
4 Women should be *objectified;* they are objects to be conquered or possessed.

It is also associated with glorifying unhealthy habits such as not seeking mental health support, working the body beyond its limits with exercise, not getting enough sleep, physical aggression leading to physical fights, risky behaviours and excessive drinking. These ideas put undue pressure on boys to conform, perform and have a long-lasting negative impact on their sense of self and mental health. It develops a rejection of empathy towards others and has been proven to build up anxiety in boys, who will struggle to manage their own feelings properly. If boys experience the pressure of toxic masculinity as children, they grow into men who are not able to express or recognise their emotions and who end up lashing out instead. It also puts intense pressure on boys to have their bodies looking a certain way, which is often ableist, unrealistic and can cause significant self-image issues.

It is, of course, highly damaging to girls too. The desire for superiority caused by toxic masculinity deeply challenges women's basic human rights and is linked to harassment and violence.

Whilst as educators we should understand this notion of toxic masculinity, we should think carefully about how and when we teach this notion to children. If the first time we teach the idea of masculinity is describing it as 'toxic', we could be doing more damage. We have to be able to redirect boys into understanding what positive masculinities are, that they are varied, multifaceted and accessible to all. It is also all about balance; it is not 'toxic' to be physically strong, only when that's understood to be the *only* way to be a man, and at the expense of looking after mental wellbeing. It is important to have an awareness of when an imbalance is jeopardising wellbeing.

We must also consider intersectionality when thinking about masculinity, meaning understanding that masculinity is not a one-size-fits-all experience and can be influenced by many intersecting factors.

*Masculinity and race.* The expectations of masculinity can differ between Black, Asian and white communities, and this will impact how individuals are able to express their own identities.
*Masculinity and sexual orientation.* The expectations of masculinity including societal attitudes will differ between heterosexual men and queer, homosexual, bisexual or transgender men. Men from the LGBTQIA+ community will have unique experiences to navigate in expressing their masculinity.
*Masculinity and class.* How masculinity is performed and understood can differ according to class and socio-economic background. There may be challenges for some in expressing their masculinity because of access to resources or financial pressure.

Educators need to prioritise dispelling dated views of 'hypermasculinity'. Instead of pointing out all the toxic male traits or defining masculinity in just one way, let's work to banish the notion of toxic masculinity so children can grow up unfazed by outdated gender stereotypes. There is no one way to be a man, and all of our actions – male or female – should be underpinned by a deep respect and empathy for each other.

## Aspirational Misogyny

Aspirational misogyny is a term used to describe boys and men aspiring to be like men famous for deeply misogynistic beliefs, actions and behaviours. They might do this by adopting some of the behaviour and attitudes of these famous misogynists – for example, being hostile towards women. Young boys may not even understand or hold the same beliefs but they see that these misogynists are [allegedly] rich, famous and powerful and it is *these* qualities they aspire to (SIA, n.d.).

The rise and prevalence of social media has provided a platform for misogynistic content to spread quickly, meaning that even if you are not searching for it, you are probably going to see it anyway. It also means that online harassment and hate speech directed towards women is more easily seen and spread.

Andrew Tate is a key example, with his influence being steeped in misogyny and gender inequality.

## Understanding and Defining Masculinities

Masculinity is not one dimensional. As educators, we need to understand the influencing factors around masculinity to help us to develop a greater understanding, a nuanced perspective and fully embrace the wide and varied expressions of it.

There is no single idea of what it means to be a man. The term masculinity simply refers to attitudes, behaviours, roles and expectations associated with being a man. It changes vastly depending on which culture or society you are in and is made up of cultural and societal norms. As mentioned earlier in the book, the whole idea of gender is constructed socially and traits are not tied to being male. It also changes throughout the ages – in Ancient Sparta the idea of masculinity centred around military prowess and physical endurance.

Positive masculinity is the idea of association traits such as emotional intelligence, empathy, respect, nurturing others. These traits foster a more diverse and inclusive understanding of masculinity, removing stereotypes and creating freedom of expression without judgement.

### Tip! 4.1

Ask your class/staff team, 'What does masculinity mean to you?' Get them to think about the values and beliefs which shape their perspectives and see if you can collectively write a definition of masculinity which is free from stereotypes. This is an interesting starting point to bounce from.

## Caring Masculinity

The development of caring masculinity is key in developing positive masculinity. This is one which is rooted in care, empathy, interdependence and challenges traditional notions of male dominance and aggression by actively participating in supportive and nurturing behaviours. By promoting the notion of caring masculinity, we can encourage boys to embrace their nurturing side and contribute to a more compassionate and equitable world. This is essentially the opposite of 'toxic masculinity', which emphasises control and power.

## Global Masculinities

Understanding what masculinity looks like differs greatly from one part of the world to another. NICRO (2023), a South African organisation which specialises in social crime prevention and offender reintegration, talks about 'collective masculinity' in Japan, which focuses on a collective identity and harmony as a group, centred around fulfilling obligations, loyalty and self-discipline. South Asian notions of masculinity are complex and vary across religions and cultures, as well as throughout history. The politics around 'manhood' are racialised and linked to a history of colonisation in this part of the world. For instance, some people connect colonisation and nationalism to dominant, violent and aggressive masculinities of upper-caste conservative Hindus today. According to Iftikhar et al. (2024), practices and experiences of masculinity for the Dalits – a group of people in India historically considered to be 'untouchables' and outcasts – have been shaped by upper castes and colonial rulers, who have traditionally exercised social control over them through aggression. In some cases, values such as discipline and abstinence, have come to the forefront as alternative embodiments of these subaltern Dalit masculinities, strongly influenced, among other factors, by the Southern Indian Hindu Sabarimala Pilgrimage (Chopra et al., 2004). There are also cultural standards which affect Muslims from this region too, where masculinity is often regarded as strength and discipline, with an understanding of communal identities of masculinity. Conversely, in Bangladesh, younger men are increasingly valuing economic independence and 'sexual agility', being more open-minded and flexible with sex and gender roles, though generally still being seen as the primary breadwinners (Iftikhar et al., 2024).

In indigenous cultures masculinity often looks totally different. An example of this is the Two Spirit identity – a gender identity which combines both the masculine and feminine – recognised by Indigenous North Americans, such as the Lakota. In land-based Canadian indigenous cultures, elders describe the men's role as being to provide for and protect the community, defending against harm. There were also male roles as healers, dancers and singers (Bidwewidam Indigenous Masculinities & Bimaadiziwin Research Project, n.d.). Pacific Islander cultures recognise the balance between feminine and masculine energies – one complementing the other, working in harmony, caregiving and mutual respect.

Conversely, in some Latin American cultures, there is the notion of 'machismo', the dominant and tough man, which is a culturally specific manifestation of the widely used term 'toxic masculinity'. There are new representations of men emerging in Latin America, shifting masculine narratives, using 'beauty and wellbeing as their conduit. This is helping Latin American men to connect with their aesthetics and feelings, deconstructing and co-creating what it means to be a man now and in the future' (Vecchione, 2022).

We can't discuss masculinity in Africa without looking at the devastating role colonisation had on the notion of masculinity in Africa. The idea of the man being the breadwinner was a colonial creation, which happened through cash crop production and the migrant labour system, targeting men specifically (Pasura and Christou, 2017). Looking at Southern Africa in particular, the apartheid regime was built on the exploitation of Black men's labour by white men, and this has lingering effects on the masculinity debate. Leaders like Nelson Mandela, who in latter years demonstrated a gentler, egalitarian and thoughtful masculinity, have been influential, but unfortunately more aggressive, dominant and patriarchal leaders have been favoured in post-colonial times (Comaroff, 2024). The continent of Africa has the highest prevalence of recorded violence against women and girls, and there is also evidence of strong links between austerity and violence. Of course, Africa is vast, and making sweeping statements about the idea of masculinity across a whole continent could be problematic – it must be recognised that in times of political, social, and economic transformation the concept of masculinity is ever-changing. Ammann and Staudacher (2020) argue that there is possibly no other continent where the depiction of men and masculinities is more homogenous than in Africa. The stereotype is one linked often to violence, dominance, the abuse of power, irresponsibility, virility, drugs and promiscuity.

In much of Africa, the man is seen as the father, protector and provider. In Zambia, there has been an increase in men's contribution to the household with housework, but as this happens behind closed doors in the home, it hasn't really changed the local notion of masculinity. There have also been societal disruptions which impact the idea of masculinity, such as war and the Ebola epidemic, resulting in the development of some new masculine ideals rooted in compassion and egalitarianism (Ammann and Staudacher, 2020).

There are also many African cultures that have emphasised the importance of collective wellbeing and value communal identity, with masculinity often being related to fulfilling family and social responsibilities. An example of this is prioritising the community over individual desires (NICRO, 2023). In addition, there are notions around respect for elders, seeking guidance from community leaders or older family members. These ideas are of course highly simplified and do not capture the full complexity of masculinity understood by the cultures mentioned, but are used to provide a whistle stop tour through differing notions of masculinity around the world.

# Tips for Developing Positive Masculinities in Primary School

So, how do we distil the above, and work on developing positive masculinities in primary school? Healthy and positive masculinity should be character-based, non-judgemental, optimistic and inclusive. Here are some key ways as educators we can support the development of positive masculinity in our settings.

### Developing Self-Awareness

Being self-aware is a skill which is important to develop when young. It supports our emotional regulation, friendships, ability to form and maintain meaningful relations and ultimately contributes greatly to our happiness. Self-awareness is the ability to understand and recognise your own feelings, motivations, behaviours and thoughts. It is about being able to tap into, and be articulate in, our own strengths, weaknesses, beliefs and values.

Understanding their own strengths and weaknesses helps children to develop a strong sense of self, build self-esteem, cope with challenges and make informed decisions. It also helps children to develop empathy for others and build strong connections with others. Learning self-awareness supports emotional regulation and executive functioning too.

## How do we Develop This in Boys?

This is a particularly powerful tool to use starting from early years, as giving all children access to brilliant learning and development opportunities in the early years is absolutely crucial in ensuring they achieve their potential. The EEF (2025) suggests the following ways of teaching self-awareness:

- *Labelling and naming.* Teachers provide labels and names for the feelings, behaviours and sensations children are feeling. This is effective both in the moment, and after the fact and can be done for both negative and positive feelings. Language like, 'I notice you are … you might be feeling …'. Example: 'I notice you are frowning and balling your fist, you might be feeling angry.' Conversely you might say, 'I can see you are being really careful and calm, you are taking deep breaths and moving slowly.' This language can also be adapted depending on the year group you are teaching. However, this strategy can be used from nursery right the way to Year 6.
- *Making links between experiences and events.* Teachers support children to make links between current situations and experiences. An example of this might be, 'Remember last week when someone had their fingers trodden on during ladders? How could we make sure that doesn't happen again?' Children tuck their hands in and keep legs closer together during the game. Another would be, 'Yesterday when we were talking during independent work, some had to finish their work during playtime. How can we make sure that doesn't happen again?'
- *Suggesting.* Teachers provide suggestions to support children to understand how to respond to their internal cues and sensations. An example of this might be, 'It can be tricky to listen if you are feeling uncomfortable. Do you need something to help you?' Teacher offers a cushion or different seat.

Wider classroom strategies might include:

- *Model, model, model.* Teachers can model throughout the day talking about how they are feeling and how they know. This is not meant as a response to poor behaviour – for example, teachers are not to say, 'You are making me feel angry' because that is totally unhelpful! It is more about telling children stories, perhaps even stories around issues you know *they* struggle with, and modelling how you overcame them. An example would be, after the morning register saying, 'Gosh my heart is beating quite fast today, I think I might be feeling a bit

anxious because there were people having a conflict on my bus this morning. I think I'm going to have some water and do some deep breaths if I keep feeling like this today.' You don't need to give any more information. Simply expressing this provides a model for children to feel comfortable to do the same. This is extremely powerful.
- *Identifying triggers.* With older children, you can do whole class teaching, small group intervention or one-to-one work with children on recognising their triggers and acting before they react.
- *Mindfulness.* This encourages children to actively notice and observe their thoughts, feelings, and physical sensations in the present moment without any judgement.

---

### Tip! 4.2

Have a mindfulness video from YouTube on the board after each transition back into the classroom from playtime. Two to three minutes will do. Give children a chance to check in with themselves and get mentally ready for the next stage of learning. This is particularly useful for classes who may have issues (around football, for example) on the playground and bring them into the classroom, causing disruption in the next learning session.

---

## Emotional Literacy and Regulation

Emotional literacy is the ability to notice, understand, express and cope with emotions. Zones of regulation is a fantastic resource for teaching children to manage big emotions. Regulation is something everyone continually works on whether we are aware of it or not – everyone encounters situations which test our limits. There are four zones of regulation and they provide an easy way to think and talk about how we feel on the inside whilst sorting those emotions into the four coloured zones.

The four zones are:

1. *Yellow – worried, silly, excited, frustrated.* In this zone, we might need to regulate/manage our energy and feelings as they get stronger. For example, if we are feeling energetic during quiet reading, it helps to use caution and take a deep breath, so we do not distract others. If we are feeling nervous before a performance, we can slow down racing thoughts and speech by doing some mindfulness. If we are frustrated, and are able to pause to take notice, we can ask for a break/cool down to collect ourselves before we say something we regret.
2. *Green – happy, focused, proud, calm.* In this zone, we can regulate by using tools and supports that keep us moving forward comfortably. For example, we might regulate by choosing to eat a healthy snack, doing some exercise, taking a break or pausing for a mindful moment. These actions are restorative and can help us proactively care for ourselves so we can move forward with ease.

3   *Red – angry, terrified, elated, panicky.* In this zone, we might need to gain a sense of control of our strong feelings and high energy by pausing and assessing if we need to regulate. For example, if we are feeling angry it may help to count to ten before we act. If feeling panicky, we could stop and use self-talk to help gain a sense of control of thoughts so that we can meet our goal. If feeling elated, such as when a team mate scores the winning goal in football, we might need to pause and take a big breath to regulate our impulse to run across the field to celebrate.
4   *Blue – sad, tired, bored, sick.* In this zone, often we need to rest and recharge. We can regulate by looking for comfort, resting or energising. If we are feeling sick, we probably need to rest. If we are feeling tired, we may need to energise. If we are feeling sad, we may need comfort. In all these situations, the common theme is around noticing the low feelings and lack of energy in our bodies and making choices to manage them.

Children need to know that all humans experience all zones – this is healthy and normal. All emotions are OK, but all behaviours are not. Emotions are complicated. They come in lots of different sizes, intensities and energy levels, which are unique to us. Zones of regulation is designed to make them easier to think about, talk about and then in turn, regulate. It provides simple and common language to talk about them, and the visuals which go alongside make the complex skill of regulation more concrete for learners. This resource is great for all learners, including those with intersectional identities affecting their school experience such as SEND and English as an additional language (EAL).

Talking through the zones with children is extremely helpful. You could ask them:

- How would you feel in each zone?
- What might happen in your body if you're feeling this way – for example, butterflies in your tummy if feeling nervous?
- What might you be *doing* if you were feeling this way – for example, being unfocused, seeming like you're not listening to instructions, pacing around?
- What could you do to regulate – for example, take some deep breaths, tell someone how you are feeling, ask for some cool-down time?
- Shall we create a list of strategies you could use if you are feeling that way? Keep the list somewhere handy, so that when the child is experiencing that emotion, they can refer to their notes. This could be in the form of a social story for younger children, and a poster for older children. Coping mechanisms could include exercise, engaging in hobbies, practising mindfulness, or seeking support from a trusted friend or mentor, engaging in activities that promote self-expression and self-discovery.

---

### Tip! 4.3

Use Widgit (a visual communication and symbol database) to ensure there are visuals linked to strategies so it is easy for the child to access, especially if they are in a heightened state of emotion. Check out https://www.widgit.com

Other ways to develop emotional literacy:

- Using books, rich texts, to teach about emotions is a great way to develop emotional literacy and regulation, empathy and emotion-based vocabulary. Some great examples are:
  - *A Big Bright Feelings Book Collection* by Tom Percival
  - *Little Mouse Is Absolutely, Completely, TOTALLY FINE!* by Sharon Hopwood and Marisa Morea
  - *The Dot* by Peter H. Reynolds
  - *I am Okay to Feel* by Karamo Brown, Jason 'Rachel' Brown and Diobelle Cerna
  - *Kairav's Colourful Feelings* by Launika Arya Raykar and Aditi Kakade Beaufrand
  - *The Red Tree* by Shaun Tan
- A strong, mental-health-based PSHE curriculum can support emotional regulation, which is crucial in promoting strong mental health, helping children manage emotions such as anger, anxiety and sadness, preventing them from developing more severe mental health issues in the future such as chronic stress, depression or anxiety disorders. PSHE should teach about mental health and strategies to notice and improve, and how to get help when needed.
- Develop strong routines in the classroom. Have a visual timetable so that children can see what is happening over the day, and remove the item from the timetable as it happens. Routines help to reduce general anxiety and create spaces that are more emotionally safe for children.
- Build in small group interventions for children who you know struggle with emotional regulation. This could be a group of boys, for example, who struggle when their team loses at football at playtime. Rather than punish children for poor behaviour after the fact, teach them how to recognise and manage those big emotions.

## Teacher CPD Around Emotional Literacy

Emotionally literate teachers are equipped to teach emotional literacy effectively. Remember, teachers/teams may need to be taught to develop this themselves in order to support the children in their case. Why not get your staff to test their own emotional literacy in a staff meeting?

Emotionally literate staff:

- Are able to reflect on their own emotions
- Ask others around them for perspective
- Don't take offence when given feedback – instead they reflect on how they can improve their practice
- Are keen to develop new skills, given the time and space to do this
- Are observant of the emotions of others around them

## Self-Care

Self-care, the act of promoting healthy habits, attitudes and behaviours, contributes to positive masculinity as it encourages boys to take care of their mental and physical wellbeing, establishing good habits for the future as they grow up. It also develops the skill of being more open about thoughts and feelings and more vulnerable in relationships. In turn, this supports boys to become more compassionate, empathetic and self-aware, ultimately leading to more fulfilling lives for them in the future.

The Education Endowment Foundation (EEF) (2025) suggests that educators teach and normalise self-care practices using the following strategies:

1. *Teach boys to name and identify emotions.* Create a safe space to openly discuss feelings like anger, sadness, frustration and happiness.
2. *Provide children with positive role models.* Shine the spotlight on positive male figures who practise great self-care – for example athletes taking care of their bodies or musicians managing stress through different relaxation techniques. You can also get male staff members in the school to model great self-care in front of children, to be a real-life role model. Provide opportunities for dads/male family members to come into the school and be involved in self-care activities such as a 'crafternoon' where they can do some mindful art with their children.
3. *Teach relaxation techniques.* Include deep breathing, progressive muscle relaxation, listening to calm music, guided imagery and make explicit links between these actions and how they support us to manage big feelings and stress.
4. *Encourage physical activity and healthy eating.* Emphasise how a healthy, balanced diet and regular exercise not only support our physical health but our mental wellbeing too.
5. *Promote positive sleep habits.* Children (and their parents/carers) need to understand the importance of a regular sleep schedule with a calm bedtime routine. Note that many neurodivergent children may struggle with sleep (e.g. autistic children) so remember to reach out to support services or a school nurse who may be able to support individual families with this if they are struggling.
6. *Promote creativity.* Be sure to encourage boys into creative activities so they get opportunities for this kind of outlet, such as art, music and a range of sports. Be explicit about the link between this and the ability to de-stress.
7. *Provide safe spaces for open communication.* Ensure that classrooms and the school more generally have spaces where boys feel comfortable talking about their feelings without judgement. You could do this through worry boxes, posters about who children can talk to if they are struggling, each child having a 'champion' (a go-to trusted adult who will check in with them regularly), building in time for pupil voice throughout the day – as simple as asking how children are feeling with a visual of a range of emotions periodically throughout the day.

## Teaching Great Communication Skills

Allyship is something that should be taught to all children, and it's particularly important to teach boys to be allies of girls. An ally is a friend who will stand up for what is right and support and defend you if you are being treated unfairly. An ally is a person who supports someone who is more marginalised than them, and is rooted in compassion and empathy.

There are several ways to do encourage allyship:

*Talk to them about inequality.* Discuss with children the different ways society treats girls and boys, and women and men. Be sure to create a classroom space where children's ideas are listened to, and get them to think critically about the different experiences of the different genders – for example, at home, at school, in intimate relationships, in the workplace. Getting children to think about this from a societal level supports children to understand that boys are not responsible for gender inequality, nor for them to feel ashamed. Rather, it's about encouraging them to think critically about society's gender expectations.

*Talk about privilege.* Children often have an innate sense of what is fair and what is unfair. Children should be taught about the notion of privilege, as this supports building allyship. This is most appropriate in upper key stage 2 (7-11 years old). Teaching them about privilege helps work towards a more equitable and just society. Privilege comes in many forms: whiteness, maleness, able-bodiedness, attractiveness, intelligence and generational wealth to name a few. A way to explain this to children is by saying privilege is a set of advantages people are born with. Get children to scrunch up a ball of paper each. Put a bin at the front of the room. Place children at different closeness to the bin and tell them they get one shot to get the paper in the bin. Explain the closer to the bin they are, the more privilege they have. Some examples of male privilege might be getting paid more than a woman to do the same job or being more likely to be hired for a job. Teach children that being a good ally means using your privilege to support others.

*Teach empathy.* Empathy is the ability to understand the feelings of another person, to be able to connect with another person's perspective and feel what they are feeling. Encouraging boys to be critical of traditional gender roles and to build empathy with each other can help boys to feel less constricted and be more able to develop positive relationships among themselves and with girls. Through stories, books, writing and reading we can build empathy skills and encourage them to put those skills into action. Try getting children to write from the perspective of a girl or woman in independent writing to get them thinking about putting themselves in someone else's shoes. Building empathy also helps children understand that they are not alone, that other people may experience some of the same experiences, thoughts and feelings as themselves, and maybe even the same problems. It helps build connections and strong relationships with one another. This is the beginning of developing young people to take part in social action later in life!

*Teach boys to model behaviour for one another.* Boys should be taught to model behaviour and challenge if someone is displaying dangerous behaviours. Teachers can do this through facilitating open and honest conversations, providing a framework for language to use giving children opportunities to practise in safe spaces and this must be embedded in the school culture and positively reinforced. An example of how to do this might be a drama activity in a PSHE lesson, where children find themselves in a scenario where someone is making a misogynistic joke, and they practise addressing it in a safe and respectful way, for example by saying, 'I don't like that joke, it's actually quite sexist.' The more opportunities children have to practise these scenarios, the more likely they are to challenge damaging behaviours in a real-life situation.

## In Summary ...

Masculinity is not a single identity. It is complex and individual, and understanding of it differs depending on which intersectional identities a person experiences. We need to nurture and teach positive masculine traits, rebrand masculinity from its 'toxic' form to more positive, healthy ideals. This will support children's development, emotional literacy and physical and mental wellbeing, ultimately leading to happier and healthier lives for our boys and men. This in turn supports safer spaces for women and girls, allowing them too to thrive and grow.

## References

Ammann, C. and Staudacher, S. (2020). Masculinities in Africa beyond crisis: Complexity, fluidity, and intersectionality. *Gender, Place & Culture*, 28(6), 759–68. https://doi.org/10.1080/0966369X.2020.1846019

Bidwewidam Indigenous Masculinities & Bimaadiziwin Research Project (n.d.) *Indigenous Masculinities Identities & Mino-bimaadiziwin*. https://ofifc.org/wp-content/uploads/2020/03/2013-Bidwewidam-Indigenous-Masculinities.pdf

Chopra, R., Osella, C. and Osella, F. (eds) (2004) *South Asian Masculinities: Context of Change, Sites of Continuity*. Women Unlimited.

Comaroff, J. (2024) African masculinity in question. *Georgetown Journal of International Affairs*. https://gjia.georgetown.edu/2024/08/09/african-masculinity-in-question

Education Endowment Foundation (EEF) (2025) Self-regulation and executive function: Approaches and practices to support self-regulation and executive function in the early years. https://educationendowmentfoundation.org.uk/early-years/evidence-store/self-regulation-and-executive-function?approach=teaching-self-monitoring-and-self-awareness

Iftikhar, I., Yasmeen, B., Noureen, N. and Iqbal, S. (2024) Beyond borders: The complexities of South Asian masculinity at home and abroad. *Kurdish Studies*, 12(3), 342–50.

Nicro (2023) *A Guide to Developing Positive Masculinity for Boys and Men*. www.nicro.org.za/images/PDFs/Positive%20Masculinities%20Workbook%20FINAL.pdf

Pasura, D. and Christou, A. (2017) Theorizing Black (African) transnational masculinities. *Men and Masculinities*, 21(4), 521–46. https://doi.org/10.1177/1097184X17694992

Plank, L. (2019) *For the Love of Men: A New Vision for Mindful Masculinity*. St Martin's Press.

Schools Inclusion Alliance (SIA) (n.d.) *Aspirational Misogyny Toolkit*. www.isaschools.org.uk/static/8acd3303-49f4-49cf-ab3e814b53825c42/SIA-Aspirational-Misogyny-FINAL.pdf

Vecchione, C. (2022) New Masculinity: Latin America, The: Future: Laboratory. https://www.thefuturelaboratory.com/blog/new-masculinity-latin-america

# 5
# Social Media and Online Safety

## Introduction

Enter the online world. This chapter discusses how misogyny is rife online, and it must be addressed explicitly through strong computing and technology teaching, but also through the wider curriculum. Sadly, owing to the nature of social media algorithms, it only takes one like of one video to be faced with endless content, ranging on the scale from 'slightly' misogynistic to full on 'manosphere' content, promoting anti-feminist and sexist views. This chapter explores online risks, how to spot and challenge them, harnessing AI for good and how to equip children with critical thinking skills to navigate the online world safely.

## What Does Misogyny Look Like Online?

The online space can be a dangerous world. It allows harmful ideas to breed, grow and develop unchecked. Algorithms amplify misogynistic and anti-feminist content, normalising harmful content for children very quickly. Misogynistic tropes and hateful ideologies then become deeply embedded in children's understanding of the world, and this in turn enters the classroom. UCL (University College London) and the University of Kent and the Association of School and College Leaders (ASCL) completed research exploring the popularisation of misogyny and hate speech online and how it puts young people are risk. They researched on TikTok and found that in just five days, there was a significant increase in the quantity but also severity of misogynistic content in their 'For You' section on TikTok (UCL News, 2024).

There is an idea called 'Moore's Law', which suggests that the capability and speed of technology doubles every two years. As an example, smartphones are over 100,000 times more powerful than the computer used for the moon landing. Communication online, which has been proven to increase feelings of loneliness in some, due to a reduction in face-to-face communication, deeply affects relational practice (Van Brunt and Taylor, 2021). There is also a rise in really aggressive communication online, and most trolls, research has found, are male (March et al., 2024). This ever-increasing number of interactions online means that children and young people are developing less and less empathy.

As adults, we are often a step behind because we do not necessarily see the same content as young people, nor use the same apps. That is all the more reason, therefore, why it is imperative that we develop our subject knowledge around hateful online content, and then teach children to recognise it, report it and think critically about it.

## The Manosphere

The term manosphere refers to an online, interconnected network of men's communities which is anti-feminist and misogynistic. It blames women for problems in society and harbours a deep resentment towards women and girls. These online ecosystems are incredibly dangerous and breed extreme attitudes related to violence and suicide. Within the manosphere, there are four main groups:

1. *Pick-up artists (PUAs)*. PUAs aim to teach men and boys different techniques to attract women, through maltreatment, disrespect and/or disregarding consent. An example of this is 'negging', which is insulting or undermining a woman in order to diminish self-confidence, making them more receptive to sexual advances.
2. *Men's Rights Activists (MRAs)*. MRAs fight for political change to benefit men, with ideas which are anti-feminist, misogynistic, male supremacist and often violent. They embrace traditional ideas of masculinity and strongly reject the principles of feminism and perpetuate traditional gender roles. They fight to change laws governing sexual assault, abortion rights and gender discrimination. Their narrative is one of victimhood and they feel that feminism has eroded their political and social capital.
3. *Men going their own way (MGTOW)*. The MGTOW community suggests that women and girls are harmful and toxic to men, so men and boys should simply avoid them altogether. Their content often suggests it is OK to date a woman but not to get into anything long term or serious such as marriage.
4. *Incels (involuntary celibates)*. This term refers to a man who struggles to find a female partner or to be sexually attractive to women, but believes that they are entitled to a relationship. Their views are extremely hostile towards women (and men) who are sexually active. Part of the philosophy is the belief that genetic factors, such as physical abilities, biological factors, bone structure, height, weight, skin colour and eye colour, predetermine their ability to be attractive to women. They believe that women are only interested in good-looking 'alpha males' (known as 'chads') and subscribe to the 80/20 rule. The 80/20 rule is the idea that the most attractive 20% of men have access to and have monopolised 80% of women. There are many examples of extreme violence linked to this group, such as mass shootings and murder (Scheele and Voogd, 2021).

The ideology of incels is different from the other extremist ideologies or online communities, because unlike the others mentioned, incels do not, they claim, *choose* their incel identity. They believe they were forced into it due to the idea of being deeply unattractive to women. This is founded on complex issues surrounding identity, feelings of not belonging and being ostracised, and the weight of societal pressure. The incel ideology is especially attractive to vulnerable young men, who have often experienced trauma, anxiety and depression. In addition, autistic men and boys are disproportionately represented in the incel community (Scheele and Voogd, 2021).

## How do Children Get Access to the Manosphere, and How Would I Know They've Accessed it?

The answer is short. Social media. There are posts and groups which operate on Instagram, YouTube, TikTok and many other platforms. Often on YouTube, the 'Watch Next' section builds algorithms known to recommend increasingly misogynistic and anti-feminist content – this is done as clickbait to keep viewers engaged. Social media has been proven to perpetuate polarisation in society by creating filter bubbles and echo chambers, spreading misinformation, and fostering tribalism, all of which support the spread of aspirational misogyny.

There is characteristic language associated with the manosphere, and it is important to be aware of it if a child uses it at school. Generalising statements about men or women are ones to look out for. Here are some examples:

- *Red pill* is a catch-all term which refers to learning the 'truth' to a supposedly difficult and hidden reality. In this context it is used to describe the nature of women and girls and the idea that feminism aims to oppress men.
- *Blue pill* is living in blissful ignorance and not taking the red pill, used to describe everyone else or 'normies' ('normal' people). The idea of the red pill/blue pill comes from the scene in the film *The Matrix*, in which Neo (Keanu Reeves' character) is offered the choice, 'You take the blue pill – the story ends, you wake up in your bed and believe whatever you want to believe. You take the red pill – you stay in Wonderland and I show you how deep the rabbit hole goes' (*The Matrix*, 1999). In this case, the 'rabbit hole' is the 'reality' that women run the world and that men are victims and must fight for men's rights.
- *Black pill*, which is specific to the incel community, is the belief that looks are genetically determined, and women choose sexual partners based solely on physical features, so being an incel is predetermined.
- An *alpha male/chad* is a man who is attractive and successful and desired by all women.
- A *beta male/cuck* is an average man who has not yet taken the red pill – he is inferior to the chad/alpha male.
- *Stacy* is the female version of a chad, an ideal woman who is only interested in chads.
- A *femoid/foid* is a 'female humanoid' – the term is mostly used by incels to dehumanise women.
- *Gynocentrism* is the idea that society revolves around and is dominated by women.
- A *thot* is a woman who has had lots of sexual encounters.

## The Manosphere: What Can we do About it?

Many of the manosphere beliefs are centred on identity, gender and sexuality. In primary schools we must act early to identify the feelings a child might have which may lead them to seek this type of content, such as low self-esteem. We must equip children with the tools to deal with the content if they do come across it. Early conversations about healthy relationships and gender relations are important so that young people do not get pulled into the black-and-white and often defeatist thinking of the manosphere.

Here are some key teaching points:

- *Strong relationships and sex education and health education (RSHE)*
  - Sex and relationships education must aim to demystify sex and sexuality. Children need to gain healthy perspectives on their own bodies, what consent means and that consent must be given freely and not under threat.
- *Caring relationships*
  - Children need to be taught the skill of care.
  - They must be taught that friendships are important, what it means to be a good friend and how to be an ally.
  - Children must understand how their friends might impact their actions or opinions.
  - Children must understand the difference between an online friend and a real friend.
- *Respectful relationships*
  - Boundaries are paramount! Children must understand their rights, their boundaries and in turn how to articulate that to others and respect the boundaries of others.
  - Children should be taught what a bystander is and about strong allyship, knowing that everyone's responsibility is to intervene and question if they or a friend are viewing damaging online content.
- *Digital media literacy*
  - Pressures from social media, friends and society could impact their thoughts and actions – digital media literacy is arguably as important as literacy.
  - Children must be shown, taught and regularly reminded how, when and where to seek support.
- *Identity and belonging*
  - In order to not feel alone, children must be taught about their own identity, how to recognise and articulate it, and furthermore feel proud of it.
  - Create a classroom where everyone's identity is celebrated and seen through display, books and teaching sequences.
- *Critical thinking*
  - Ask critical thinking questions in a calm and positive way.
  - Children need to be taught to seek first to understand if someone has a differing opinion to their own.
- *Oracy*
  - Children need to be able to use their voices to discuss, build and challenge, and this can be done by creating classrooms which put oracy at the centre.

- Provide opportunities for children to talk through their ideas, to actively listen to the ideas of others and respond based on what someone else has said, rather then simply adding their ideas.
- Provide children with opportunities for exploratory talk – sharing ideas towards a shared understanding.

All of the above need strong adaptive practice for autistic children and children with additional learning needs.

# Pornography

The ability to access hardcore and unregulated pornography has dramatically increased over the past few years. There are many adolescents who seek out pornography, but there are also children and young people who stumble across it accidentally. The Children's Commissioner for England found through research that by the age of nine, 10% had seen pornography and 27% had seen it by the age of 11 (Children's Commissioner, 2023). Children exposed to pornography for the first time at age 11 or younger are more likely to have significantly lower self-esteem as young adults. Pornography can lead to unrealistic expectations around body image, relationships and sex. In addition, research has found that viewing pornography is linked to developing sexually aggressive tendencies, endorsing rape myths and developing deeply misogynistic, degrading and dehumanising views of women and girls (Van Brunt and Taylor, 2021). There is also a normalisation of sexual violence found in online pornography, which plays a huge role in understanding sex and relations. Moreover, pornography is not confined to dedicated websites – children and young people have access to this kind of content through social media such as X (formerly known as Twitter), Instagram and Snapchat. In addition, children may receive or view explicit content from other children who have accessed it. Remember, it only takes one child, in one class, to see something inappropriate and share it, for all children in the class to know about it.

The NSPCC found in their research about children and porn that:

- 53% of boys believed the pornography they had viewed was 'realistic' compared to only 39% of girls
- 90% of children have been exposed to pornography online by the age of 14
- 79% of young people encounter violent pornography before they reach 18 years old and frequent users are more likely to engage in physically aggressive sex acts
- 33% of children who have viewed online pornography were exposed to it accidentally, while a quarter were sent it by a friend (Internet Matters, 2025).

The impact of viewing pornographic content on children is enormous.

- *It promotes unhealthy relationships.* Viewing pornography at a young age distorts children's expectations and understanding of relationships and sex. They may see acts of disrespect and violence and are led to believe these are normal parts of relationships. They may also believe that there is something wrong with *them*

if they do not want to take part in these acts, rather than realise some of these acts are actually abusive.
- *It negatively impacts mental health.* For children, viewing pornographic material may shape their attitudes about what it means to be a man or a woman, skewing their understanding of masculinity and femininity, as well as negatively impacting their body image. Boys may develop harmful attitudes towards women and for girls it may cause pressure to live up to the expectations created by pornography and their body image. For both and for gender nonconforming children this can lead to anxiety and depression.
- *It can cause early sexualised behaviour.* Exposure to pornography from a young age can affect children's development and lead them to display early signs of sexualised behaviour. This may develop into problematic or abusive sexualised behaviour later in life, which is harmful both to the child and to the people it is directed at.

## Pornography: What can we do About it?

All staff need to be trained in the signs to look for in children's behaviour which may indicate that they have been exposed to inappropriate content online. This needs to be shared with the parent/carer community too.

Vigilant practice is the key. Look out for:

- Children displaying negative and changing attitudes towards women and girls, seen through children's play and/or interactions in the playground
- Use of sexualised language
- Knowledge and understanding beyond their years

---

### Tip! 5.1

Take a look at Hackett's continuum and Sexualised Behaviour in Children resources on the NSPCC website and the online training, which is inexpensive but brilliant. Hackett's continuum is used to understand children's sexualised behaviour, taking account of the context, age and development of the children. Behaviour is categorised into three sections: developmentally typical, problematic and harmful. Inappropriate behaviour may be one-off instances of generally consensual sexual behaviour, whereas problematic behaviour may be something more compulsive, involving an imbalance of power and developmentally unusual (NSPCC, 2025a). For example, it is developmentally typical for toddlers to have curiosity and touch each other's and adults' body parts, but it wouldn't be for a ten-year-old to do this. This continuum helps practitioners to understand children's actions in context, which supports safeguarding actions.

Strong online safety teaching from the early years is extremely important because it is likely that children of all genders may find it difficult to speak to adults about topics which may be personal and embarrassing to them, such as their bodies, sex and relationships. This can make reporting online misogyny difficult.

## Artificial Intelligence (AI)

Artificial Intelligence describes the ability of machines to perform tasks that normally require human intelligence. This is the broad term for a range of technologies that use algorithms to solve complex problems. Many people have virtual home assistants such Alexa, Siri or Cortana – is it a coincidence that their default voices are female? I wonder what this says about perpetuating the 'good housewife' or feminine subservience.

Generative AI (gen AI) is a type of AI which produces new content like text and images. There are lots of benefits to gen AI which can support children's learning and wellbeing, such as support through helplines (e.g. Kids Help Phone – an online mental health service) and customised learning experiences.

However, like everything, generative AI tech also poses lots of risks to children. An NSPCC report (2025b) into this found that gen AI is being used to extort, bully, sexually harass and groom children. It also found that deep fake personas can be created (by either adults or children) which use video and voice generation technology. These deep fakes can depict children doing or saying things they wouldn't in real life, and may change their physical appearance. This can make them a target of humiliation or blackmail. Gen AI can also collect behavioural or personal information to target children's algorithms with dangerous and harmful content and adverts. For example, a child searching 'AI girlfriends' may then be exposed to misogynistic content.

## AI and Bias

AI reflects the gender bias from the offline world. This gender bias happens partly due to the dataset – if there are not as many women contributing, it creates gaps in the AI's knowledge meaning bias errors occur. Machine learning is human-led, which means human bias is incorporated in the data and AI system. This is also true of the intersection of race. There is also a gender digital divide which creates a data gap, reflected in the gender bias in AI. In other words, AI creators build their own biases into AI data, which can then widen and perpetuate gender bias. An example is searching for terms such as 'doctor' and only getting male images, whereas searching 'nurse' would reveal female images. Searching for AI pictures of 'women' gives outcomes of white and thin women automatically. UN Women (2024) found that AI-powered services and technology will continue to lack diverse gender and racial perspectives, with that gap resulting in bias and lower quality of services if current trends continue.

A *Guardian* investigation by Mauro and Schellmann (2023) found that when AI algorithms analyse images posted on social media, they decide what to suppress and what to amplify. Many of these algorithms show gender bias. Some of these tools, designed by leading companies such as Google and Microsoft, aim to identify pornographic visuals and violent content, so that social media companies are able to block it. They are also designed to detect how sexually suggestive an image may be and suppress contentious images. The investigation found that pictures of women doing everyday things like working out are tagged as more sexually suggestive than photos of men doing the same thing, meaning that these algorithms suppress countless images of women's bodies, damaging many female businesses and further perpetuating societal disparities. Another example was pregnant bellies or women breastfeeding being classified as 'racy'. This hinders women's self-expression, access to healthcare information and finances. This gender bias promotes misogyny online and reinforces negative attitudes and views of women.

Whilst as educators we may feel deeply concerned about the risks posed by AI, we have to recognise that technology like this is revolutionary, and it will undoubtedly play a significant role in children's future lives and work, so we need to learn about it and find ways to keep children safe. Banning children from using gen AI is not the answer. We need to *teach* them and develop strong safety measures to protect them from harm.

## AI: What can we do About it?

Teachers can support children to understand the concept of AI bias and its potential consequences by talking about it and critically thinking about real-world examples of bias in AI systems. We should teach children to think critically about AI data and safely incorporate AI into the curriculum in an ethical and responsible manner.

AI is a tool. Who uses the tool (and how) depends on how fair, equitable and positive the outcome. This is what children need to be taught. Giving children opportunities to both learn about and understand the technology that will inevitably shape their future, teachers can inspire deep passion for creativity and innovation, and spark interest in digital literacy, critical thinking and problem solving.

> **Tip! 5.2**
>
> Check out Kapow Computing Curriculum – there are units on AI for upper KS2 (9-11 year olds) which are good for challenging pupils' thinking and understanding around AI.

A great way to introduce AI into your classroom is to explore concepts *with children*. By doing this, you may build new strategies for teaching complex topics, and foster a tech-savvy learning environment, developing children's understanding of AI too. This will help to personalise lessons, stay abreast of digital trends and prepare children for a future where AI will play a large role. This will develop your teaching practice – if done correctly – and enhance pupil outcomes.

Here are some tips:

- *Start simple*. Teach children what AI is, a tool which follows commands, and link it to their everyday lives.
- *Build AI into play*. Children could act as AI robots and must follow commands to complete tasks. Through this level of interactive play, children can understand the basic AI model.
- *Link to ethics*. Children are able to understand the idea of ethics from the early years and the idea of fairness all the way to Year 6 when children can take part in debates. Give children questions to discuss such as, 'Is AI a good or bad thing for the world?', 'Will AI create or take away more jobs?', 'Should machines make

decisions for people?'. Discussions around these ideas will help to develop critical thinking and oracy around this topic.
- *Incorporate storytelling.* Storytelling is a really great way to illustrate concepts around AI, and a good way to explain it to young children.

There are a variety of tools for teachers, designed to save time and reduce workload. These include:

- Using tools to create modelled writing, being sure to add in elements such as 'British English spelling conventions'
- Using tools to create characters or settings to supplement creative writing – this is a good prompt for children to be able to use keywords to develop characters/settings to look like what they pictured in their heads
- Developing maths problems for pupils, to challenge and be explicitly linked to skills taught in the lesson

An inclusive coding curriculum is one that is designed to appeal to all genders. To do this you must use examples and projects that are relevant to all genders. In order to truly eliminate gender bias within AI, we need more women and girls to be part of designing it. We need to inspire girls into STEM and ICT careers. In order to do this we need to foster curiosity by providing early exposure to science, technology and maths through hands-on activities. We need to highlight successful women in STEM fields as role models, and supportive and inclusive environments.

---

**Tip! 5.3**

Check out A Scientist Just Like Me – a project by the Primary Science Teaching Trust which is designed to raise awareness of diversity in science-related jobs and to give illustrated examples of a variety of STEM careers. Their website has a series of slideshows telling the story of an individual scientist or person working in a STEM career. They are designed to challenge gender stereotypes linked to STEM careers and can be used in class or as a whole-school assembly.

---

Did you know the person who wrote the world's first machine algorithm – the first ever computer programmer – was a woman, Ada Lovelace? Here are a few examples of inspiring female role models in coding:

*Reshma Saujani.* Reshma is the CEO and founder of the organisation Girls Who Code, which aims to close the gender gap in technology through education.
*Carol Shaw.* Believed to be the first ever female video game designer, she was integral to designing the Atari 2600 vertically scrolling shooter River Raid for the company Activision, and when at Atari she developed lots of classic video games such as 3-D Tic-Tac-Toe and Video Checkers.

*Susan Wojcicki.* Often thought as the most powerful woman in tech, she was CEO of YouTube and has been a big advocate for inclusion and diversity within the industry.

> **Tip! 5.4**
>
> Check out the organisation Code First Girls, which works to close the gender gap in tech through free coding education for women and girls. Girls Who Code is another organisation, one that offers a gaming experience which empowers users to create characters through code that better reflect them and the diversity of their communities.

## Influencers

The definition of an influencer is someone who has a large following on social media. They promote products, ideas and behaviours to their followers. There are influencers for every topic imaginable, from gaming to cooking to sports. Influencers can have a greatly positive effect on children, if they are promoting self-esteem and healthy habits. However, conversely there are lots of influencers who promote deeply ingrained misogyny, which is extremely damaging to children, particularly if they associate the views and ideas with wealth, respect and power. The content influencers share is most often their own personal thoughts and opinions. This means that often information being shared isn't always factual or fact checked. This in turn means children are at risk of being exposed to misleading and false information as content influencers' posts are often not moderated. Content can be misinformation (incorrect information that the influencer believes to be true) or disinformation (deliberate lies). Some influencers promote messages that objectify and sexualise women, sending messages that women are primarily valued for their appearance, which leads to a harmful culture of harassment and discrimination.

The NSPCC (2023) reports that UK schools have found more and more boys using online influencers as role models, including content which promotes violence against women and girls, and hate speech.

You would have to be living under a rock not to be aware of Andrew Tate and his self-proclamation of being a 'misogyny influencer'. I almost do not want to give him any more publicity than necessary. His violent and heinous opinions – and actions – coupled with his declarations of riches beyond wildest dreams, can attract vulnerable boys who wish for the same money and power as him.

This level of misogyny is a form of extremism, and that children are accessing these videos should be a red flag. Many people link awful crimes such as the murder of three girls in Southport in July 2024 to extreme misogynistic content (Block, 2025). The Home Office has said that extreme misogyny will be treated as a type of extremism under new government plans (Catt and Rose, 2024) – let's hope they stick to this.

## Female Influencers

There are female influencers who also perpetuate damaging and misogynistic views, such as Kendal Kay who espouses the 'SAHG' lifestyle. SAHG stands for 'stay-at-home girlfriend', where a woman's only role is to serve her boyfriend and look beautiful. With a large focus on self-care and beauty, many criticise this culture, which has arisen on TikTok and Instagram, as it undermines women's independence and creates vulnerabilities and emotional dependence. The key idea is that to be seen as desirable, young women behave in a way which is often derogatory to themselves or other women. They promote this idea that gender roles should be clear and rigid, and sometimes glamourise the 'olden days' as being happier times.

This is linked to the 'pick me girl' culture, where girls and young women behave online in ways which are derogatory to other women or themselves in order to be more desirable to men.

## 'Pick me' Girls

The concept of 'pick me' girls is one in which a girl embraces the male gaze, and places high value on the interests, habits and activities of straight, cisgender men – often to their own detriment. They want to be seen as 'wifey' material, and the aim is to garner male attention and distance themselves from other women.

## The Power of Influencers: What can we do About it?

Here are some of the things we can do about this.

### Know the Red Flags

Knowledge is power. Educators must keep up to date with online harms through regular training. This can be tricky if you do not have an expert on your team. If this is the case you need to invest in some regular training for staff. Websites such as NSPCC and Internet Matters offer brilliant resources for both educators and the parent community, which can be used as training resources, staff meetings, or even mini training in staff briefings. Children mentioning the names of certain influencers, or manosphere acronyms or words is a safeguarding matter, and should be treated as such. Report it, meet with parents, put actions in place to support that child.

### Curiosity not Judgement

As we know, safeguarding and the welfare of the child is paramount. Educators need to ensure they are listening to children's worries, concerns or just opinions. If there are red flags, they need to be met with curiosity not judgement. Seek first to understand. Often children who are accessing harmful content are:

- Left unattended using devices and stumble across it
- Shown content by older siblings or peers
- Searching for it due to feelings of curiosity, loneliness or anger

We need to consider how and why the content was accessed, and ensure same-side conversations are had, rather than judgemental ones. This way, we can put in teachable actions to teach both the child and parent to be safe online.

## Engage don't Dismiss

Power battles between educators and children never work. If a child is demonstrating extreme misogynistic views, engage with them and have a conversation, ideally not in public. Get to the bottom of why they think what they do and how they accessed that information. Most often, children will be repeating what they've heard someone else say without really understanding the depth of it. Teach them about equality and why it matters – relate it to them, their lives, their families. Ask them to reflect on the women and girls in their lives – for example, a mother, sister, grandmother, aunts, teacher, friends. Contextualising their thinking helps them to readjust the lens.

## Teach Responsible Behaviour and Make Time for Children to be Heard

Critical thinking and accountability are important – children need to understand that their voices will be heard, and they must judge when is and isn't an appropriate time to offer views unprompted.

An assembly about women's rights, for example, is not a time to shout out harmful opinions about women, but you can create time and space by saying to all children, 'If there is anything anyone wants to talk about after this please let me know.' If harmful views are shared then, you can then seek first to understand, redirect and have a same-side conversation about how to consider things more critically. Same-side conversations are ones where you can physically sit by the side of the child, reducing pressure and the feeling of confrontation for a child – it also means listening more than talking, and supporting the child to feel like you are on their side, you are listening, not judging and ultimately wanting to help.

## Use Male Allies

Ensure the men working in your school are demonstrating powerful male allyship by being explicit about views and beliefs about what it means to be a male, show emotional vulnerability, and break gender stereotypes.

> **Tip! 5.5**
>
> Think about the interventions in your school and who runs them. You may, for example, have a male mentor who supports your older boys if they are struggling. Think about how you can use these sessions to break gender stereotypes - you could have a cook and chat mentoring group run by a man, or a weightlifting/boxing mentoring group for girls only. These subtle changes send powerful unspoken messages to children about gender stereotypes.

## Consider Your School Culture

Do you unknowingly perpetuate gender stereotypes? Look at the language, events and activities at your school, as well as policies and practices such as uniform, toilets, assumptions and expectations and consider whether you may unknowingly be reinforcing rigid views of gender.

Ask yourself:

- Is your uniform policy gendered, or can anyone wear a skirt or trousers or shorts?
- Are there gender-neutral toilets?
- All teachers should be empowered to teach some PE – is PE taught solely by men?
- Are there gender-challenging images across the school – in lessons, presentations, on display boards, on your website, etc.?
- Is there shared accountability for all pupils to speak out and be listened to when they feel there is sexism? Sometimes if only one gender group receive a consequence – for example it is the boys in the class who broke a rule, therefore it is the boys who receive a consequence – children may say that you, the teacher, is being sexist. Go back and explain the behaviours leading to the consequence and the accountability associated so that they fully understand and don't feel they are on the receiving end of sexism themselves. You must take the time for children to be listened to, so that you can teach and redirect. If children are dismissed they stop trying to be heard and seek other ways to be seen and heard – for example, online.
- What do the roles in your school say about your school and your culture?

# Working with Parents: A Healthy Digital Diet

Social media algorithms target children's vulnerabilities – for example feeling alone, angry or out of control. They then gamify this content and expose children to extremist content. As children scroll through this, they get a dopamine hit and it feels entertaining and may confirm their bias – and so the cycle begins. We can tackle this with a healthy digital diet, a bit like when we talk about balance within our food diet. Educating parents and carers is key – schools must promote wider awareness of these algorithmic processes alongside teaching parents what a healthy digital diet looks like:

- Consider the different types of screen time and digital content children are engaging with, how much of it is consumed and understand how it can become 'ultra-processed' because of algorithms (UCL News, 2024)
- Consider how this impacts children's mental and physical health

## Provide Bespoke Support

The impact of misogyny and accessing harmful content online will affect different children in different ways.

> ### Tip! 5.6
>
> Create a spreadsheet database of local organisations that support, teach and mentor children who are at risk. We must work holistically – keeping children safe is multi-agency work. A child accessing inappropriate or harmful content online is a safeguarding concern and should be treated as one.

## Be Explicit

In lessons – whether computing or PSHE – explicitly teach what misogynistic content is, how to spot it and how to challenge it. It is imperative to provide children with opportunities to learn about both their rights and the rights of others, as well as the impact of misogyny and the harm it causes. In Chapter 8 you will find a range of lesson ideas and plans you can use or adapt.

> ### Tip! 5.7
>
> Be intersectional. Remember that often it is children with a range of marginalised intersectional identities who are more at risk – for example autistic boys may be at an increased risk of accessing harmful content online, as they may be more likely to experience feelings of not being understood. Adapt your materials, lessons and support to ensure it is accessible to all. This could be through visuals, positive uses of adaptive technology, scaffolding, differentiated resources, positive reinforcement and collaboration with parents.

## Bring Parents into the Conversation

Provide regular information and support for parents, bringing in speakers and experts to run coffee mornings and online sessions. Remember to have an intersectional approach to this. It may be the parents who are unable to attend coffee mornings during the working day, who have children at risk, so provide options, provide translations, listen to them and their needs and provide suitable training. Consider your vulnerable child register – look at the parents of the children and think about how you can provide training which will reach your most vulnerable, not your most *available*. Often, when we do parent courses or coffee mornings, they occur during times that are not accessible to working parents for example – think about how you can combat this – start with asking parents who might benefit from it what times/days work best for them.

## In Summary ...

The online world can feel chaotic. Children will often be one step ahead in terms of their understanding of apps, the internet and influencers. However, we must put the effort into ensuring that we are clued up on the risks; that we take a stance of curiosity – not judgement; and that we actively teach critical thinking to spot and challenge online misogyny.

## References

Block, I. (2025) Portrait of a killer: How the Southport murders are part of a new pattern of violent terror. *The Standard*. www.standard.co.uk/news/uk/southport-murder-stabbing-axel-rudakubana-b1206358.html

Catt, H. and Rose, C. (2024) Misogyny to be treated as extremism by UK government. *BBC News*. www.bbc.co.uk/news/articles/c15gn0lq7p5o

Children's Commissioner (2023) *Evidence on Pornography's Influence on Harmful Sexual Behaviour among Children*. https://assets.childrenscommissioner.gov.uk/wpuploads/2023/05/Evidence-on-pornographys-influence-on-harmful-sexual-behaviour-among-children.pdf

Internet Matters (2025) How online pornography impacts children. www.internetmatters.org/issues/online-pornography/learn-about-it

March, E., McDonald, L. and Forsyth, L. (2024) Personality and internet trolling: A validation study of a representative sample. *Current Psychologyl*, 43, 4815–18. https://doi.org/10.1007/s12144-023-04586-1

Mauro, G. and Schellmann, H. (2023) 'There is no standard': Investigation finds AI algorithms objectify women's bodies. *The Guardian*, 8 February. www.theguardian.com/technology/2023/feb/08/biased-ai-algorithms-racy-women-bodies

NSPCC (2023) The influence of influencers: What you need to know about online influencers. available at: www.nspcc.org.uk/keeping-children-safe/online-safety/online-safety-blog/2023-05-16-the-influence-of-influencers

NSPCC (2025a) Understanding sexualised behaviour in children. https://learning.nspcc.org.uk/child-abuse-and-neglect/harmful-sexual-behaviour/understanding#article-top

NSPCC (2025b) *Viewing Generative AI and Children's Safety in the Round.* https://learning.nspcc.org.uk/media/ikxlpzt2/viewing-generative-ai-childrens-safety.pdf

Scheele, R. and Voogd, A. (2021) The incel phenomenon: Exploring internal and external issues around involuntary celibates. Radicalisation Awareness Network (RAN). https://home-affairs.ec.europa.eu/system/files/2021-08/ran_cn_incel_phenomenon_20210803_en.pdf

*The Matrix* (1999) [DVD] Directed by Lana Wachowski, and Lilly Wachowski, United States, Warner Bros.

UCL News (2024) Social media algorithms amplify misogynistic content to teens. www.ucl.ac.uk/news/2024/feb/social-media-algorithms-amplify-misogynistic-content-teens

UN Women (2024) Artificial intelligence and gender equality. www.unwomen.org/en/articles/explainer/artificial-intelligence-and-gender-equality

Van Brunt, B. and Taylor, C. (2021) *Understanding and Treating Incels: Case Studies, Guidance and Treatment of Violence Risk in the Involuntary Celibate Community.* Routledge.

# 6
# Working with Parents and Carers

## Introduction

Much toxic behaviour may be influenced by home life and influences outside of school – it is for this reason that working with parents and carers is essential. This chapter suggests ways in which you can work with your parent and carer community to raise awareness, address issues when they arise and empower them to challenge and promote positive and healthy views of women and girls. When we discuss 'parents' in this chapter, we are talking about all who take up a parental role, recognising that for some children this is parents, for others this may be carers, grandparents, aunts, uncles or other family members.

## Proactive, not Reactive

In order to get the best outcomes for children, schools must work holistically to support children. Working with the parent community is absolutely key in this – you can make wonderful progress at school but if children go home to differing viewpoints or misunderstanding what the school is trying to achieve, progress stops. Schools that interact effectively with parents are more successful and this significantly impacts children's educational success. If your communication with parents is purely *reactive* – communication solely when something has happened at school such as attendance, behaviour incidents or safeguarding issues – it is difficult to build trust. Schools must work to be *proactive* with the parent community. This includes finding ways to involve and teach parents what their children will be learning in school and *why*. It includes running a range of events to engage parents and in addition thinking carefully about communications going out to parents at the appropriate time.

It is also important to consider intersectionality when thinking about the 'how' and 'when' with the parent community. Know your community. If you only run coffee mornings after morning drop-off, you exclude most working parents and parents of older children whose children travel to school alone (often *these* are the parents you most need to engage with). Never describe parents as *hard to reach*. The school is hard to reach *for them*. Think about your community and plan events accordingly. If you have a large community from one nationality, for example, consider catering with food from that nationality. Likewise, if you have a large community from one religion, plan events around that – for example, having an Eid celebration (if you have a large Muslim community) or an Easter Bonnet parade (Christian), or running your own Holi Colour Festival (Hindu).

Think carefully about ways you can communicate with parents and families with whom English is not their first language. There are a few ways to do this, depending on your community:

- Offer translated versions. Be wary of simply dropping it into an online translator, however, when communicating sensitive information.
- See if you have any staff members who speak the same language, or your local authority may have a translation service you could use.
- Find another parent or family who speak the same language and can support with translation.
- Run an event with that community to build links between parents who speak the same language – often parents can feel ostracised or like they don't belong if they struggle to speak English, especially if they have joined mid-year, it may mean that not only do they struggle to communicate with you, but also to make relationships with other families. If you have a new family to the school who speak Pashto for example, run a mini event with your Pashto families so that you can build relationships between families. I have never seen a parent smile so much as I did when I did this at my school – connection is so powerful.
- If you do not have anyone else that speaks the same language, contact another local school to see if you can find families/staff members who do speak the language, or pillars of the community – for example, religious institutions (if relevant). If all else fails, seek to build online links outside of your locality.

Consider other groups of parents and carers who may feel that school is hard to reach – for example, parents of high need children. Consider running events for this community of parents, so that they too can build relationships with other parents who also have high need children. Again, drop off and collection may feel like a challenging time for this group of parents. It may be, for example, that parents of children with education and health care plans (EHCPs) might find the start of the day really challenging, and to get children ready for school and to arrive on time may be a struggle. This may mean that they are often late. Think about the message and the interactions they experience from school daily. Is it a daily 'telling off' from your office staff or attendance officer who are working on improving attendance for all? Whilst we are all working on this, schools need to have a 'seek first to understand' stance on punctuality. It is often significantly more difficult for a parent of a high need child to arrive on time. Treat them with kindness and understanding, and most importantly, no judgement. No amount of tutting or telling off is going to make the morning routine easier for a parent with a high need child. Offer strategies to support – home visual timetables, or even a staggered start where appropriate. Running events for parents of high needs children can be powerful. Parents may feel like other parents in the class of their child cannot understand their daily lives, but parents of other high need children can. Planning these events, which could be as simple as, come in, have a biscuit and a hot drink and simply chat allows parents to share worries, challenges and successes with someone who understands. This can be transformative for families, making them feel that they are not alone. When parents build friendships with others, they are then in turn more likely to attend whole-school events.

> ### Tip! 6.1
>
> Events with food are much better attended than events without! So, get to the shops or get cooking and baking. Food brings people together.

## To Matter

It is extremely important that parents and carers feel like they matter. This is beyond just feeling like they belong; you can feel like you belong to a community but not feel like you matter. Mattering is linked to feeling significant, like you and your voice are valued. This idea of mattering is fundamental to being human.

First you need to get parents through the door and build relationships and trust with the school, *then* once trust is built, you begin to speak about the curriculum, the school's vision and any particular projects you're working on. Be sure to plan a timetable of events at a range of times – after drop-off, home time, evening events online. This works to include everyone.

## Parent-Teacher Association (PTA), Parent Governors and Parent Reps – What's the Difference?

Schools will be set up in different ways, and there may be different official parent groups, or there may be none! It is important to know the difference, and furthermore ensure parents know the difference, so everyone knows where they stand.

Some schools will have an active PTA (some an *over*active PTA!), and some schools no PTA at all. It is really important to be clear on what the remit of the PTA is. The PTA is a group of parents and teachers who aim to raise funds, strengthening the school community. Money raised is usually spent on things that the school budget does not cover. The PTA *is not* a spokesperson for the parent community nor a body to hold the headteacher to account – its remit is fundraising.

Parent governors are elected members of the school's governing board, voted in by parents of registered pupils. Their role is to bring a parental perspective to the decision making of the governing body and ensure the views of parents are considered. Likewise, a parent governor *is not* a spokesperson for the parent community nor a role to hold the headteacher to account – the remit is to bring parental voice to the governing body.

As a leader/teacher at the school you can put in place a system of parent reps. We live in a world now where most parents have WhatsApp, and often there are school or class WhatsApp groups. This is not managed by the school and shouldn't be! There is too much to do without managing adults and their WhatsApp groups! However, if you appoint parent reps, you can ensure communications to parents are widespread and in line with the school's aims and vision. For example, you could appoint two parent reps for each class. When you send letters home with information about key events, ask the parent reps to post them on the WhatsApp groups and/or speak to parents in the playground. This is a really effective way of ensuring all parents have access to school communications. Particularly if you choose parents whose experiences and identities may help them support more marginalised parents with receiving and understanding communications, this can be really powerful. Appoint them by approaching parents who you think would be suitable. Let them know it takes no time out of their day (as this can often be the barrier to parents feeling that they want to be involved!).

### Tip! 6.2

Here's an example poster for parent reps:

### Parent Reps Wanted!

I am looking for *2-3 Parent Reps* per class. The Parent Representatives group is a vital connection between the school and the parents and carers. It aims to keep parents informed of what's going on in school, share key communications and it is hoped that, through an improved understanding of how and why things are done, parents are encouraged to remain active and informed partners and participants in the life of the school.

Being a Parent Rep is a role in which you can make a real contribution to our school and, we think, one you will enjoy. Here are some of the key tasks:

- Ensure *key messages* from school are shared with the class groups (I appreciate that sometimes messages can get lost at the bottom of book bags!). This might be a reminder of key events coming up, trips, homework, etc.
- *Support the teacher* in organising year group cake sales etc. when needed.
- *Coordinate a card from parents* at Christmas and at the end of the school year for the teacher and classroom assistant.
- Arrange occasional social activities for parents in your class to build friendships between parents and to make the organisation of class activities easier.
- *It is not designed to take any additional time.*
- *You do not need any special skills!* We also welcome anyone who can speak more than one language.

If you are interested, you can find [the Headteacher] on the playground or drop the office an email and we can chat about it.

## Curriculum

It is really important that parents know what is being taught and how. This supports parental understanding of key issues, particularly related to how the school works to eliminate misogyny and promote positive masculinity, and most importantly, why.

There are many ways to do this effectively. Here are a few ideas:

- Ensure the class curriculum is on the school website. This allows parents to access it with ease. Some websites even have a translate button, allowing for parents with different languages to access it too.
- Ensure that on this class curriculum, you include the school's vision. If your curriculum vision is, 'our teaching is anti-racist, anti-sexist, anti-homophobic and anti-ableist', ensure that statement is on *everything*! The website might be wonderful, but it is unlikely that parents searching for their child's curriculum are going to navigate the whole website and also read the curriculum vision page – make it easy for them!
- Have a half-termly newsletter per class, mapping out the upcoming term's learning. Include links to videos for parents to watch if they want to learn more. It is really useful to include PSHE and RSE teaching material videos so parents can access the kind of content that is being shared and taught. A parent might not understand how you teach about consent at a Year 2 level, so this really helps. Remember to send out paper copies to parents who you know may not be able to access this online.
- In the summer term, once you know which staff will be teaching each class in the new school year, organise a Meet The Teacher Day when teachers can discuss the curriculum for the year and talk through any key messages.
- Speak to your local authority/diocese/academy trust – there may be a PSHE coordinator who offers free workshops for parents. This is particularly useful for topics such as puberty, sex education and consent.

## Events to Support the Curriculum

There are lots of different events schools can run for parents to discuss and/or learn about key information in relation to tackling misogyny, promoting positive masculinities and online safety. Here are some ideas:

*Online safety workshops.* Online safety is a safeguarding issue, and as discussed in Chapter 5 it is imperative that parents have a chance to learn about the risks and what they can do about them. The ChildNet and Internet Matters websites offer free presentations for parents, which can be led by a staff member. You can run the workshops yourselves, or you can ask for charities or local organisations to come and speak with parents about this. Ask your local authority safeguarding lead who may have some contacts with local organisations. Some great organisations are Kidscape, the NSPCC, Social Switch and the UK Safer Internet Centre.

*Awareness days.* There are a number of awareness days throughout the year, which you can observe and fundraise for, raising awareness of key issues surrounding misogyny, such as:

*White Ribbon Day,* 25 November. This is an international day for raising awareness of violence against women and girls. Why not get your whole community to wear white (including staff and parents)? Run an assembly and parent information event on the same day to raise awareness. On the White Ribbon website, you will find child-friendly assembly resources which are centred around kindness, empathy and tackling violence and aggression. If you sign up as an ambassador school, you will get some free posters and business cards, which you can put up and give out. You could also run a poster competition for children and buy prizes such as white ribbon pin badges or lanyards, meaning you are donating to the cause and raising awareness amongst the pupil community.

*Safer Internet Day,* second Tuesday in February. This is to raise awareness of online safety issues and promote responsible use of the internet and how best to support children with their digital literacy. To celebrate this, you can find age-appropriate resources on the UK Safer Internet Centre website for assemblies, activities and quizzes, etc., and you can register as supporters to showcase your commitment to online safety. You can invite parents to a parent session on online safety and give tips for supporting children to use the internet at home safely while informing them what is taught in the computing curriculum at school.

*LGBTQIA+History Month,* February. A reminder that the fight against misogyny is intersectional, and traditional notions of masculinity are more often than not incredibly homophobic. Celebrating LGBTQIA+History Month is a great time to learn about the rich and diverse histories, herstories and their stories! It is a time to raise awareness of LGBTQIA+history and struggles and foster an understanding of these varied and diverse identities, in turn helping combat misogyny by challenging gender stereotypes and promoting equality for all. Representation matters. You may also have some same sex families in your school, and celebrating this sends a strong message to the community that you are inclusive, and that everyone is welcome. This in turn will support parental engagement in the school.

*Neurodiversity Celebration Week,* March. Reflecting back on understanding that many teenagers and men who commit violent crimes against women and who are involved in the manosphere are neurodivergent (Hymas, 2024), this week is a really important one, to remove stigma around neurodiversity, practice neuro-affirmative strategies and provide meaningful role models to children. While of course not all autistic boys go on to be misogynists, some neurodivergent men do commit misogynistic crimes, so there is definitely a conversation to be had around adaptive teaching of empathy, kindness and fairness for the neurodiverse community. In addition, both autism and ADHD have strong hereditary components. As with LGBTQIA+History Month, representation matters.

*International Women's Day,* 8 March. This is a global event, celebrating the amazing achievements of women. Consider the most appropriate way to celebrate this in your setting. What you don't want to do is send the message that we only celebrate women's achievements on this day and not the rest of the year and that this is a tokenistic celebration. Make it clear to children that we celebrate women all year round. Likewise, you will inevitably have questions such as, 'Why don't we celebrate International Men's Day?' Explain to children that we celebrate this special day as we still live in a world where there are inequalities for women, and we want everyone in this world to have the same opportunities, no matter if they are a girl or boy.

*International Men's Day*. Historically this is not something that has been celebrated in schools, as arguably, every day is international men's day as men hold societal power. However, given that most suicides are men, prisons are filled with men and boys underperform girls at every stage of education (Lee, 2021), I wonder if we are entering a new era when schools should celebrate this day, and use it as a platform to celebrate and promote empathy, positive masculinity, kindness, respect, and explore role models who challenge the mainstream idea of what it means to be a man. You could base the day on Ben Brooks' book *Stories for Boys Who Dare to Be Different*.

---

**Tip! 6.3**

Why not include information about the awareness days in your weekly newsletter. You could include questions that children may ask their parents, and empower parents with how to respond.

Here is an example for International Women's Day:

## Spotlight on: International Women's Day

International Women's Day is a specific day dedicated to the successes and advancement of women worldwide.

Marked by millions of people on 8 March, International Women's Day celebrates the political, economic, social and cultural achievements of women and is a call to action to fight for gender equality.

International Women's Day provides an important platform to engage with communities, reflect on progress and commit to positive action. Participation in International Women's Day ensures that progress towards equality remains on the global agenda and positive action prevails.

This day has a powerful history of collective action, with many groups, countries and bodies having contributed actively to its evolution resulting in it being a widely celebrated and highly visible worldwide event receiving significant mainstream awareness in a wide variety of ways.

## What are the aims of International Women's Day?

International Women's Day can mean different things to various groups, yet the overarching aims of this day are to:

- Celebrate women's achievements through appreciating and recognising the contributions of women across various fields, highlighting their successes and influence both throughout history and in the present day.

- Foster solidarity among people of all genders in support of gender parity and women's rights worldwide.
- Raise awareness of gender inequality by shining a light on persistent issues like lack of representation in leadership roles, gender-based violence, the gender pay gap and unequal access to opportunities and education.
- Call to action for equality by encouraging people (individuals, communities, and organisations) to take steps towards creating a more equitable and inclusive world for women.
- Donate and fundraise for women-focused charities, and elevate the visibility of their work.

### Why Don't we Celebrate International Men's Day?

Children sometimes ask this question and it can be a tricky one to articulate. Many people argue that men already hold significant societal power and don't need a dedicated day to address issues they face, while women historically have faced greater systemic inequalities requiring more focused attention on their challenges; this can be seen as a matter of addressing historical gender imbalances. This is comparable to Black History Month or Disability History Month (whilst recognising the struggles are unique and different).

## Communication: How to Guides

Parents can often transfer their own gender biases to their children – for example, girls may be treated as fragile or praised for their beauty while boys may be encouraged to always be strong and be praised for their physical strength. Through biases like these, children are taught to behave according to these socially 'accepted' norms of their gender, which can be harmful to their emotional and social development.

'How to' guides are really useful for the parent community, to explain the learning or events you are celebrating, and explain the 'why'. Timing is everything. You don't want to bombard parents with endless information, but well-timed, easily accessible information can be really useful to parents. You could have one themed newsletter per term, aligning with celebrations the school is taking part in, or with what is going on with the world. Often parent complaints come from a place of not fully understanding what the school is doing or offering, so these act as a support to developing a shared understanding of the school's offer. Here are some examples.

### Parent Guide on ... How to Talk to Your Children About Gender

Gender can feel like a complicated issue to talk about, especially when children are asking questions about some of the things they have learned, or seen on TV or social media. You can help them navigate this complex world – we have put some information together to help you do so.

## What is Gender?

Gender refers to the characteristics of girls and boys, men and women – these are socially constructed.

## What is Gender Equality?

Gender equality is when people's access to rights or opportunities is unaffected by gender. Gender inequality can be seen in a number of ways. Here are some examples:

- Jokes, stereotypes, unacceptable use of language and objectification
- Harassment, threats and verbal abuse
- Emotional abuse
- Financial abuse
- Violence, rape, sexual assault or physical abuse

## How do I Talk to my Child About This?

Have open conversations. Look for moments to talk to your child about equality. This could be after watching something on TV, or perhaps when something pops up on your social media and you use it is a prompt to have a discussion.

- *Ask first.* Ask your child what they think about an issue. Ask what they already know or believe. Prompt further by asking, 'How do you know?, 'Why do you think that?' or, 'What might someone with a different view think?'
- *Listen and validate.* Listen to your child and their experiences and opinions. Let them explain to you what they feel and model respect for them even if you have different views.
- *Read and chat.* Read books that challenge gender norms together such as *Gender Swapped Fairy Tales* and *Books for Boys Who Dare to Be Different*. Chat about the characters and their actions as you read.
- *Raise questions.* Speak to your child about what they're seeing on social media and the influences around them. Challenge any damaging stereotypes you come across. This can help your child understand why they're harmful and support them to think critically about what they see.
- *Be reflective.* Share your own experiences and knowledge with your child – e.g. 'When I was at school people used to call me a tomboy all the time, but there's lots of different ways to be a woman ... right?'
- *Go deep.* Talk to your child about consent and respect. Help them to understand body boundaries and what is and isn't OK. Ask them when you greet them if they want a hug or a high five for example. This models asking for consent for body touch even from a trusted adult. Talk to them about things like banter and explain when that may become bullying or harassment. Be open and honest. Help them to feel confident discussing those things with you. Make sure they know what to do if they ever feel uncomfortable or are in trouble, and who they can speak to.

### How do I Promote Gender Equality in Our Home?

Your daily actions and habits, even the smallest things, can support promoting gender equality in your home. Here are some ideas:

- *Allow your children to play with whatever toys they like*, regardless of their sex. All play helps children to develop life skills.
- *Be a role model.* Show examples of gender equality in the home. If you have a partner, try to share jobs equally and let your children know this. It is everyone's job to help with things like cooking, cleaning, gardening or washing the car.
- *Challenge stereotypes.* For example, girls and women are often represented by sexist and racial stereotypes. Take time to look at inspirational and powerful people of all genders and ethnic identities from history and celebrate their strengths. Teach your child about their identity, and to be proud of who they are.
- *Celebrate diversity.* Explore a range of different cultures with your child using books, films, the local community and music.
- *Promote self-care and encourage self-confidence.* Teach your child to understand and respect their body and to be aware of how things like social media might affect how they think they should look.
- *Remember that all human beings have feelings and need to express these feelings.* It's OK to show emotions, whatever your sex or gender identity. Teach them that all emotions are OK, but all behaviours are not.
- *Accept your child.* Give your child space and freedom to be whoever they want to be. Don't assume or predetermine their sexual orientation or perceptions of their own gender. Avoid judgement. Let them know you will always be there to guide them if they need you.

### What if They Ask me Questions I Can't Answer?

You don't have to know all the answers. In fact, there's power in saying, 'Hmm. I am not sure about that, let's find out.' You can then seek answers together – for example, by doing a search on the internet – and you can also use this as an opportunity to model being critical about the results you find. For example, don't simply take the first answer that pops up. Consider the source of the information and talk your child through this.

### Parent Guide on ... LGBTQIA+ Inclusive Teaching

It's important to talk to your children about discrimination. At [school name] we actively challenge and fight against all forms of discrimination. Just like Black History, we learn about and celebrate diversity in all its forms throughout our school year and throughout the curriculum. We teach equality and social justice for all races, genders, sexualities, religions, abilities and more. We are required to do so by the Department of Education. We are proud of the curriculum we teach and its impact upon developing well-rounded citizens in our young people. The purpose of this newsletter is to give you some information to discuss at home with your family.

The rainbow is a symbol of hope. Many people throughout history have used this flag, from LGBT, to NHS Clap for Carers, to its use in religious history. This flag is a symbol of hope, promotes inclusion and equality and most of all ... happiness.

## Tackling Homophobia

Homophobia is dislike of or prejudice against gay people. It is important to understand that in our society, lots of different people exist. We actively teach understanding, social justice and equality. We teach these through our varied curriculum, where we challenge phobic views of groups of people within our society (and community). We challenge stereotypes and learn how to think critically about issues. We tackle discriminatory language and have zero tolerance for bullying in all its forms. We educate against discriminatory language and teach acceptance.

The Lesbian, Gay, Bisexual and Transgender community have been through many struggles throughout history and it is important to learn about this struggle, the fight for change and the continued journey towards equality, in the same way we learn about fights for race equality and much more. This is always done in an age-appropriate way.

We teach children that families come in all different shapes and sizes: two-parent families, single-parent families, two mums, two dads, living with grandparents, living in foster care and many more. The glue that keeps families together is love. This week, to celebrate LGBT History Month, we will be having an assembly entitled 'Same love, different families' where we will explore different family make-ups.

## Let's Talk About Definitions

Ask yourself – do you truly understand the definitions of gender and sexuality? Here are some definitions quoted from the LGBTQIA Resource Center (2025), to help and discuss with your children whenever the time is right.

- Pronoun: A word that can take the place of a noun or noun phrase, such as he/him, she/her, they/them.
- Gender identity: A sense of one's self as trans, genderqueer, woman, man, or some other identity, which may or may not correspond with the sex and gender one is assigned at birth.
- Gender dysphoria: Used to describe when a person experiences discomfort or distress because there is a mismatch between their sex assigned at birth and their gender identity. This is also the clinical diagnosis for someone who doesn't feel comfortable with the sex they were assigned at birth.
- Transgender: An adjective used most often as an umbrella term and frequently abbreviated to 'trans'. Identifying as transgender, or trans, means that one's internal knowledge of gender is different from conventional or cultural expectations based on the sex that person was assigned at birth.

- Gay: A sexual and affectional orientation toward people of the same gender.
- Lesbian: Someone who identifies as a woman, whose primary sexual and affectional orientation is toward people of the same gender.
- Non-binary: A gender identity and experience that embraces a full universe of expressions and ways of being that resonate for an individual, moving beyond the male/female gender binary.

## Empathy Through Literacy

Empathy means understanding how someone else feels. Here are some great children's books which explore issues of gender, stereotypes and teach about different families and LGBT history:

- *And Tango Makes Three* – Justin Richardson and Peter Parnell
- *All Are Welcome* – Alexandra Penfold
- *Pride: The Harvey Milk Story* – Rob Sanders and Steven Salerno
- *Queer Heroes* – Arabelle Sicardi
- *Rainbow Revolutionaries* – Sarah Prager

### Tip! 6.4

Internet Matters has lots of conversation guides for parents, for talking to their children about their online life. Link these on your school website and have some printed in the school office in case they may be useful for parents.

# Engaging Dads and Male Family Members

As discussed throughout the book so far, tackling misogyny is not a women's issue, it's an everyone issue. Often, the parents attending school events tend to be women. There are lots of reasons for this. However, schools need to work hard to engage dads and male family members also, in order to build a strong community around gender equality. It is important for boys to see male family members showing support of these issues and can really help to make a difference.

Why not try other ways to engage dads and male family members such as:

- Sports events – parents vs staff are always fun events. Football matches and mini marathons are good ways to bring in parents

- Fitness classes
- Have a male staff member run a dads/male family members group – coming together at a mutually convenient time and chatting about issues is a great way to get people involved in school
- Crafternoons – run events where parents can come and spend an afternoon crafting with their child and learning about the school

---

**Tip! 6.5**

Parent voice matters. Be sure to regularly seek parent voice on key issues, appropriate times for events and listen to feedback where applicable. Give parents enough notice to attend events. There is no point organising events with a couple of weeks, notice. They will not be as well attended as they would if you gave them longer to plan around work and/or childcare commitments.

---

## When Incidents Happen

No matter how proactive we can be with parent communication there will inevitably be times when you will need to be reactive – meeting with parents about behaviour incidents. It is important that sexism and misogyny are taken seriously at school, and when an incident occurs parents are invited in to speak about it. When describing an incident, it is important to be clear and non-judgemental, explaining incidents as they happened and naming the behaviour. For example, if a Year 6 boy slaps a girl's bottom, ask the parent to come in, describe the incident and name it as sexual harassment. Sexual harassment can occur between children, and it's vital to take such incidents seriously, offering support and addressing the underlying issues. Peer-on-peer sexual harassment is unfortunately shockingly commonplace in secondary schools, so we want to do everything in our power to stamp this out on a primary level so that children understand this is not acceptable. The only way to do this effectively is to work with parents to ensure the zero-tolerance message is clear.

## In Summary ...

Strong relationships with the parent community are crucial in keeping children safe, fulfilling the school's vision, eliminating sexism and misogyny and promoting positive masculinity. Engaging both parents and teachers in developing these relationships is vital in order to create the best holistic learning environment for children. Develop a community where all feel like they matter, that they are valued, and that they trust the school. Be transparent, teach parents what you're teaching children, empower them with the language and tools to speak with their children about key issues and listen when they ask for help.

# References

Hymas, C. (2024) Incels 30 times more likely to be autistic, study finds. *The Telegraph*. www.telegraph.co.uk/news/2024/02/14/incels-more-likely-to-be-autistic-involuntary-celibate/?ICID=continue_without_subscribing_reg_first

Lee, R. (2021) Should we celebrate International Men's Day? History, controversy & significance. *Morson Talent*. www.morson.com/should-we-celebrate-international-mens-day

LGBTQIA Resource Center (2025) LGBTQIA Resource Center Glossary. https://lgbtqia.ucdavis.edu/educated/glossary#g

# 7
# Working with the Wider Community

## Introduction

The wider community is a powerful tool for schools and teachers – knowledge is power and working together in a holistic way supports children and parents to be educated, feel safe and ask for help from the community around them outside of school. This chapter includes tips for how to work with the local community and build great relationships, as well as using the expertise of other practitioners in the community to keep children safe.

## Strength of Community

It takes a village to raise a child. There are so many different people playing a part in improving the health and welfare of children. Learning about and working with your wider community leads to improved learning, stronger families and healthier communities. Engaging parents and the wider community in schools helps to improve educational outcomes for children and keep them safe. A particular focus for many schools is involving parents who find school hard to reach. Schools, parents and the community need to work together to promote the health, wellbeing and learning of all pupils, supporting the development of an anti-misogynistic culture. When working in this way, schools are better able to respond to the social health-related needs of pupils. This in turn raises academic achievement, improves behaviour and reduces school exclusion rates too.

The Equality Act 2010 gives protection against discrimination to anyone with a protected characteristic, such as age, disability, gender reassignment, marriage and civil partnership, pregnancy and maternity, race, religion or belief, sex or sexual orientation. It also places a duty on public authorities, including schools, to support equality of opportunity, eliminate discrimination and foster strong relations between different groups of people. Communities cannot be cohesive when discrimination and inequality exist, meaning that actions to eliminate discrimination and further equality should be an integral part of a school's work to promote community cohesion (NASUWT, 2025).

So let's first establish what we mean by community. This has a number of dimensions:

- The individual school community, including pupils, staff, governors, parents/carers and users of the school's facilities and services
- Wider school communities, including networks, partnerships and clusters of schools
- The local community, including the immediate neighbourhood, the city/town and the local authority where the school is located
- The UK community, the national community
- The global community, around the world!

To carry out effective work on tackling misogyny in schools and violence against women and girls, there will be a range of tiered responses, depending on the incident. These tiered responses will actively involve members of the community, so it is important to build strong partnership links with groups and organisations in order to build a robust culture of safeguarding. The tiered responses are:

- *Universal response (focus on prevention for all children)*. Challenging gender roles and stereotypes, challenging language and practices that support inequality, curriculum review and input, particularly around PHSE and/or RSE, lessons on knowing what abuse is and how to seek help
- *Targeted response (additional support for some children)*. Responding to patterns of incidents of unacceptable attitudes/behaviour directed towards an individual, wellbeing assessments and meeting individual needs
- *Specialist response (individualised support)*. Child protection procedures

In the previous chapter we discussed working with the parent/carer community. In this chapter we will explore the wider community and how strong partnerships can support the tackling of misogyny in primary schools. Schools will need to operate across each of these dimensions. In areas where the community is less diverse, schools will need to seek out opportunities to enable pupils to interact with people from a range of backgrounds, which could be done through seeking connections online. In addition, it is helpful if all schools can at least start to identify ways pupils might engage with different communities across the UK and globally.

## School Communities

When thinking about developing a curriculum or projects around anti-misogynistic practice, it is worth reaching out to local schools, or other schools within your cluster/network/trust to see if there is anyone else that wants to join you. There is strength in unity. Working as a group also lessens the workload on one school or one teacher, if indeed you are developing new topics around gender, positive masculinity and anti-discriminatory practice.

For example, why not reach out to your local school and find another teacher teaching the same year group, who wants to collaborate on planning and/or ideas. Conversations with other practitioners will be inherently useful, sharing reflections and data on children's behaviour and language around gender, who takes up the most space in the classroom, attitudes towards women and girls, etc.

Remember that the first step in the Education Endowment Foundation implementation cycle is around engaging, uniting and reflecting in order to adopt the behaviours that drive effective implementation (EEF, 2024). You could:

*Plan.* Each plan a six-week PSHE unit. Share and compare notes. You could get the children from each class to share their key learning with each other through a showcase, or even via a Zoom if the timetable is too tight to meet in person.

*Track behaviour incidents.* Examine your data on the attainment and progress of different groups of pupils, the nature and number of any bullying and/or prejudice-related incidents and pupil behaviour, including rates of suspension and exclusion. Take a baseline analysis of the number, and type of behaviour incidents occurring in each of your classes. Put in place a term's intervention of zones of regulation/emotional literacy for boys who are repeatedly involved in behaviour incidents, and then do another analysis after a period of time (two terms minimum) and compare data. If you begin to see an improvement, you then have some evidence to replicate on a larger scale across the school/s.

*Start a campaign.* Children across two or more schools could start a campaign against violence against women and girls. Children could plan and deliver assemblies, lessons to other classes, parent sessions, welcome visitors to the school, run fundraising events collectively for a greater good.

*Learn together.* Economies of scale mean it is often most cost effective to pay for training and CPD for a larger group of practitioners, than it is for small teams. Why not team up with another school, or group of schools, and have a larger-scale CPD session or INSET session. This then splits the cost of training across groups of schools, making it kinder on already-tight budgets.

## The Local Community

There is often so much amazing work that goes on in local communities that in schools we are unaware of. Most, if not all local authorities will have a strategy to end violence against women and girls and gender-based violence. Do your research. Find out what the strategy is and who is leading on it. Reach out to them – find out more information and what your school can do to get involved. In addition, many local authorities will have a forum or working party made up of practitioners. This is a great opportunity to build strong links with the community and find out exactly what work is going on. In community groups or VAWG forums, the aim is to share good practice, raise awareness of VAWG in the locality and enable practitioners to stay up to date with local, regional and national policies that impact on the sector.

> **Tip! 7.1**
>
> VAWG forums often meet during the working day. If you find a local one and want to attend, be sure to think about and explain the wider impact for the school and the children when you request time to attend, particularly if you are a class teacher.
> Something like …
>
> I would like to request [time and date] out of class to attend the VAWG forum online. I want to learn about the local strategy to prevent VAWG and find out more about local organisations which can support in particular women who have been victims of domestic abuse. This information will better help us to safeguard our most vulnerable families and offer more holistic support.

## Dealing with a Gender-Based Violence Incident

Supporting a child who has been the victim of gender-based violence is best when it is holistic, multi-agency work. If a child were to make a disclosure, staff would need to immediately follow child protection procedures. Beyond that, in order to support that child in school, developing strong relationships with local support services (for both child and parent) is really important, and of course liaising with your DSL/social care/police to make sure all support is appropriate and in line with recommendations. As an example, you may have local organisations who offer complex case therapy free of charge for victims of gender-based violence, or parent/carer groups. There may be organisations who offer weekend respite or in-school mentoring. Do your research, and hold professionals' meetings, bringing together expertise of key practitioners across the local area to ensure the child and family gets the support they need.

In this instance follow your school's child protection procedures and contact the police (if necessary). In addition, the designated safeguarding lead (DSL) may be able to find local organisations/community support that can help the child and family also – be sure to speak to your (DSL) about this – or if you are the DSL, speak with the local authority and/or police about this first.

## Supporting Children Who Have Witnessed or Experienced Domestic Abuse

Domestic abuse is any type of controlling, threatening, violent or coercive behaviour between people who are, or who have ever been in a relationship, regardless of gender or sexuality. It can also happen between family members (NSPCC, 2024). It includes:

- *Physical abuse*. Being kicked, punched, hit with objects
- *Coercive control*. Being told what to do, where to go and/or being isolated from family and friends

- *Emotional abuse.* Being ridiculed, intimidated, harassed, undermined, sworn at or threatened
- *Rape and sexual abuse.* Either within the relationship or made to have sex with others
- *Harassment and stalking.* Being followed repeatedly, being spied on, receiving regular unwanted communications or receiving unwanted gifts
- *Tech-facilitated abuse.* Having phone, emails or online messages monitored and/or deleted, receiving constant messages and/or phone calls, having location tracked and monitored (NSPCC, 2024)

Bearing witness to any of these behaviours has a profound effect on a child or children and being exposed to them is in itself child abuse. Children are affected both directly and indirectly. Seeing or hearing them can cause significant trauma to the child and if they do not get the support and care they need it can undermine their basic need for security and safety.

An example of support for mothers and children once there is no further risk of domestic violence to them is DART (domestic abuse recovering together). This is an NSPCC service which supports children and their mothers who have been survivors/victims of domestic abuse and do not live with the perpetrator any more. This service is often available through local authorities, and is recognised by the Home Office. It is a ten-week programme that supports communication between the child and mother, and aims to rebuild relationships. Try searching online for your local council and domestic abuse services to see what they are able to offer you.

Engaging with local community partners could form a part of both universal and targeted approaches supporting children and families. Staff in schools can call on a range of support from education, health and local authority services (as well as additional organisations and services) in both prevention of – and early intervention relating to – gender-based violence.

In particular, schools can seek engagement with and support from their local area multi-agency violence against women and girls partnership and youth services. This partnership will lead to local strategic action to prevent and tackle the issue of violence against women and girls.

Where there is a risk of significant harm to the child, staff in schools should always invoke child protection procedures rather than seeking multi-agency voluntary support.

## Local School Nursing Services

School nursing services are well positioned within schools to support children with their health and wellbeing. School nurses work with children and families from when they start school at four years old up to 19 years of age and are usually linked to a school or group of schools, building a link between school, home and the community. They can help by signposting or referring to other services.

If a child has witnessed or experienced domestic abuse, or any other forms of gender-based violence at home, school nurses can often help. School nurses know that domestic abuse and violence have a major impact on the health, emotional, intellectual and social development of a child and have a major impact on the family. Identification of need and early intervention work with families often significantly reduces the risk of ongoing harm and is important for the health and wellbeing of the child and families affected.

They will complete a holistic assessment of the child's health and wellbeing needs and provide the necessary support. Where more specialised input is required, school nurses can make referrals to other services, ensuring children receive the appropriate care.

School nurses may be able to support with interventions developing parenting skills, support families and help to strengthen relationships between parents, carers and children. This can have long-lasting prevention benefits and can prevent child abuse whilst also improving child behaviour, reducing children's risks of involvement in abuse later in life. Other programmes may support the development of life and social care skills and can build social and emotional competencies in the child. Some other effective interventions may include mentoring programmes, community-based interventions, and early intervention programmes as well as interventions as part of the school curriculum, for both children and parents. There may also be advocacy programmes and support agencies such as local Independent Domestic Violence Advocacy (IDVA), Sexual Assault Referral Centres (SARCs), Multi-Agency Risk Assessment Conferences (MARAC) as well as Refuge provision and Criminal Justice interventions to support and work with perpetrators of domestic abuse too (DfE, n.d.).

## Police: Walk, Talk and Do

The police offer Walk and Talks, sometimes called Walk, Talk and Do. These are open to women (aged 18 years+) and are a chance to walk through troublesome or worrying areas within the local community alongside a police officer and discuss safety and experiences in these areas, with the hope of meaningful change and better understanding. The aim of a Walk and Talk is to build conversations and trust between police officers and members of the public, and have concerns listened to and taken seriously.

There may be a particular spot around your school which feels unsafe. It could be an alleyway, a road prone to crime or a public space like a park or green which is not well lit during the winter months and feels unsafe. Why not organise a Walk and Talk with the police, and ask parents and their children (where appropriate) to come along and discuss feelings of safety and suggestions for improvement. You could even invite your local councillors to attend so that they can support and prompt police to make changes if needed.

## Local Council

Local councils are a group of elected councillors. Councillors work with local people, community groups, schools, businesses and other organisations, to agree and deliver on local priorities. Their role is to serve and represent everyone in the ward where they are elected. In addition, some are also appointed to additional roles in the council, for example being a cabinet member. The role aims to bring people together. Building relationships with local councillors can help schools by advocating for their needs, fostering community partnerships whilst also teaching children about democracy, citizenship and politics.

## Religious Institutions

Depending on where your school is located, you may have at least one, if not a number of religious institutions nearby. These could range from churches, to mosques, to synagogues, to temples, to gurdwaras and more. Making links with them can foster inclusivity, promote understanding of different faiths and cultures and support implementation of anti-discriminatory practice.

The best way to do this is to pop in and introduce yourself! Invite leaders to school events – the summer fair, Eid celebrations, Christmas shows, etc. Getting different religious leaders involved in schools promotes a culture of respect and acceptance, celebrates interfaith diversity and dialogue, and supports some families who may find school hard to reach. It serves as a way to develop strong intersectional inclusive practice.

## Charities and Organisations

There are a number of charities and organisations that do amazing local work with families in need, women and children who have experienced gender-based violence, or who support the mental health of men in order to tackle violence against women and girls. Find out what types of charities and local organisations work in your locality. Here are just a few that do incredible intersectional work and might be available to your school community:

*White Ribbon.* White Ribbon is a charity which engages men and boys in ending violence against women and girls. Its aim is to prevent men's violence against women and girls by addressing the root causes. The charity works with boys and men to change harmful and long-established attitudes and behaviours around rigid gender norms and masculinity that in turn perpetuate inequality and violence.

*Beyond Equality.* The organisation works to equip men and boys with new perspectives, starting the process of community change, personal development and working for gender equality.

*Voicebox.* The organisation promotes gender equality and positive masculinity through workshops, assemblies and projects designed to empower children, tackle toxic masculinity, promote healthy masculinities and challenge misogyny.

*Karma Nirvana.* Karma Nirvana runs the national Honour Based Abuse helpline, and is a specialist charity for survivors and victims. It works to support, empower and educate those impacted by honour-based abuse so that they can live free from fear and abuse. It also runs training for frontline professionals and practitioners, and campaigns for change, working with policy makers and parliamentarians.

*Galop.* Galop is a helpline and anti-abuse charity supporting LGBT+ people who have experienced violence and abuse, including domestic abuse, sexual violence, hate crimes, so-called conversion therapy, honour-based abuse and other forms of abuse. It offers evidence-based training, bespoke to your setting.

*Respect.* Respect is a charity aimed at keeping survivors safe and stopping perpetrators of domestic abuse, whilst offering perpetrators meaningful opportunities to change. It does vital work with young people who cause harm, ensuring its work is pioneering, collaborative, accountable and respectful. It offers interventions to support perpetrators in the early stages of abuse and those displaying highly harmful behaviours, recognising that a range of interventions is required to meet the needs of perpetrators. The charity conducts research, engages in practice and pilots new interventions, accredits services and influences policy.

*Refuge.* Refuge is a charity that supports women and children who have experienced abuse. Some of its community services extend to men also. It offers a range of support for women who have experienced gender-based violence. Refuge staff specialise in providing practical and emotional support, part of a coordinated multi-agency response to meeting the needs of victims and survivors of all forms of VAWG, including domestic, sexual, technology-facilitated and economic abuse and so-called 'honour'-based violence, as well as coercive control, stalking, FGM, modern slavery and human trafficking, prostitution and forced marriage.

*Women's Aid.* Women's Aid is a charity working nationally to end domestic abuse against women and children. It provides life-saving services across England while building a future where domestic abuse is not tolerated. Women can get support with housing, safety planning, dealing with police and more.

*Rape Crisis.* Rape Crisis is a feminist charity working to end child sexual abuse, rape, sexual assault, sexual harassment and all other forms of sexual violence. It has 37 member centres nationally and works to deliver specialist services to those affected by sexual violence and abuse, aiming to educate, influence and make change. It does this by fighting for victims and survivors to have access to specialist support, raising awareness about the prevalence and impact of sexual violence and abuse, challenging rape culture and influencing change in all aspects of public policy relating to sexual violence and abuse.

*Southall Black Sisters.* Southall Black Sisters is a charity that highlights and challenges all forms of violence against women and girls, empowering them to gain control over their lives, asserting their human rights to justice, equality and freedom. It provides holistic advocacy services predominantly for and from Black and minoritised women, to live free from fear, violence and abuse. It also provides advice for women who have no recourse to public funds, providing a safety net and access to refuge or safe accommodation, helping them escape from abuse, prostitution or human trafficking.

*Imkaan.* Imkaan is a Black and minoritised feminist organisation, working with and for other Black and minoritised violence against women and girls 'by and for' organisations. It centres anti-racism as a key component in tackling VAWG. It works with issues such as domestic violence, forced marriage and honour-based violence at local, national and international level, and is partnered with a range of organisations, improving policy and practice responses to Black and minoritised women and girls.

*End Violence Against Women.* This is a group of feminist organisations and experts from around the UK, working to end violence against women and girls in all forms. It takes an intersectional, anti-racist approach to transform the political and social systems that enable violence against women, whilst driving social change through campaigning and shaping policy, and challenging the wider cultural attitudes that can tolerate and normalise abuse.

*Respond.* Respond is a charity that supports people with learning disabilities and autistic people who have experienced abuse, violence or trauma, providing trauma-informed psychotherapy and advocacy for survivors of sexual and domestic abuse. It also supports people to navigate the criminal justice system and develop understanding around this.

> ### Tip! 7.2
>
> Create a database of local organisations that can support schools, children or families, either through preventative training, workshops and curriculum development or through early intervention and/or support through negative experiences. Keep this as a live document, shared with staff and add to it each time you learn about or work with different agencies or organisations.
>
> Columns in your database should include information such as:
>
> - the name
> - services offered
> - for whom
> - contact details
> - notes

## Accreditation

Working towards an accreditation for anti-discriminatory practice is a great way to engage the community in a commitment to quality education, enhance credibility with pupils, parents and the wider community and ensure continuous improvement through rigorous assessments and standards. Awards and accreditation send a strong message to the school community and future families about what your school stands for and its ethos and vision.

Of course, it needs to be aligned with your vision, and you need to share the 'why' with your staff team, pupils and parents in order to get buy-in. You also need only do one at a time! You don't want to be working towards numerous accreditations as this reduces the focus and importance of the work. Here are a few suggested accreditations, which lend themselves to great anti-discriminatory practice:

*Rights Respecting Award.* Led by UNICEF, this is used across the UK. The scheme recognises schools for embedding children's rights into their vision, policies and practices, based on the UN Convention on the Rights of the Child. Schools have to demonstrate that children's rights are at the heart of school life with a strong culture of respect, equity and participation. There are three levels: bronze, silver and gold. The award is rooted in the principles of equality, dignity, respect and anti-discriminatory practice. Schools receive the accreditation from UNICEF UK after demonstrating that they have reached the three RRSA Strands and any other requirements through a detailed evidence form and a school visit when representatives of UNICEF talk to teachers, children, school leaders, parents and governors.

*UK Feminista Award.* The UK Feminista: Action Award recognises schools that have taken outstanding action by implementing a whole-school approach to tackling sexism and sexual harassment. As a school you will need to evidence the work that has been undertaken to combat sexism and sexual harassment and demonstrate the impact this has had on children and the school community. There are three categories of the award – bronze, silver and gold.

*White Ribbon Award.* The White Ribbon Accreditation is a programme which supports organisations to implement and develop a three-year action plan to address violence against women and girls, focusing on promoting gender equality, empowering men as allies and raising awareness.

### Tip! 7.3

Don't start an accreditation mid-year. Align the accreditation to targets in your school development plan. Get the whole-school community and local community involved in implementing it, including your school council which can support raising awareness in the pupil community. Have a regular feature in your newsletter/website indicating how you are getting on with the accreditation. This will raise its profile and ultimately make it more successful.

## The Global Community

We are also part of a global community, and the work on eliminating violence against women and girls isn't solely local and cannot be done in isolation. The United Nations is an international organisation of 193 countries committed to maintaining international peace and security, developing friendly partnerships between nations and promoting social progress, better living standards and strong human rights. In order to do this, the UN has 17 Sustainable Development Goals (SDGs), as a universal call to action to protect the planet, end poverty and make sure all people enjoy peace and prosperity by 2030. The goals are interconnected – the key to success for one will involve tackling issues with another.

These are:

- Goal 1: No Poverty
- Goal 2: Zero Hunger
- Goal 3: Good Health and Wellbeing
- Goal 4: Quality Education
- Goal 5: Gender Equality
- Goal 6: Clean Water and Sanitation
- Goal 7: Affordable and Clean Energy
- Goal 8: Decent Work and Economic Growth
- Goal 9: Industry, Innovation and Infrastructure
- Goal 10: Reduced Inequalities
- Goal 11: Sustainable Cities and Communities
- Goal 12: Responsible Consumption and Production
- Goal 13: Climate Action
- Goal 14: Life Below Water
- Goal 15: Life on Land
- Goal 16: Peace, Justice and Strong Institutions
- Goal 17: Partnerships for the Goals

(UN, 2025)

Gender equality and women's empowerment is one of those goals – goal number 5. It won't come as a surprise that we are not on track to achieving this goal by 2030. In fact, the UN reported in 2023 that it will take 286 years to close the gap in legal protection and eliminate discriminatory laws and 140 years to achieve equal leadership representation in workplaces. These stats are quite maddening. However, we can only do what is in our sphere of influence to chip away at this issue, which is raising awareness and educating.

To incorporate the global community in your work to tackling misogyny you could:

- Fundraise for key awareness days such as The International Day for the Elimination of Violence Against Women, observed on 25 November
- Ask your school council to name a charity working in this space, and then all fundraising for the year is raising money for this particular charity – such as Action Aid or Malala Fund
- Audit your curriculum and see how your school is doing its part to raise awareness about the 17 SDGs
- Link up with another school abroad – share good practice, create pen pals, develop relationships. If you are a faith school, your religious institution will likely have links with schools in different countries. If you regularly have PGCE students training with you, ask the associated university if they have links with schools abroad, or failing that, ask your school community if anyone has partnerships with schools in different countries.

> **Tip! 7.4**
>
> When working to create global partnerships, ensure that your narrative isn't 'Western world = good, non-Western world = bad', as this will perpetuate stereotypes rooted in colonisation. Make sure that links do not reinforce pupils' perceptions and stereotypes about people living in poorer countries. Work to ensure that the relationship between the schools is equal and the school in The UK is not simply seen as the source of knowledge, expertise and money. Make sure that relationships between partner schools are mutually beneficial and aim to achieve equity by setting shared goals.

## In Summary ...

It really does take a village to raise a child. There are endless benefits to developing strong partnerships and working collaboratively with your community, especially in the work to eliminate violence against women and girls and promote positive masculinity.

These partnerships can provide opportunities to pool resources and ideas, including knowledge and expertise, give care and support for those in need and provide opportunities for students to interact and work with people from a range of backgrounds. Relationships must be mutually supportive, leading to benefits for both pupils in the school and the wider community. Ensure your work with the wider community is mapped out in your school development plan, with clear objectives linked to your priorities, and how it can be sustained over time. It is important to clarify who is responsible for the different aspects of this community work, drawing on people's interests, expertise and knowledge. Don't fall into the trap of pressuring certain staff members to take on responsibilities just because they come from a certain background themselves – for example, global majority or from a faith group.

To create a true culture of safeguarding, we must involve wider communities – both local and beyond – in order to power the fight to eliminate violence against women and girls and support those affected.

## References

Department for Education (n.d.) Health visiting and school nursing programmes: Supporting implementation of the new service model: No. 5: Domestic violence and abuse – professional guidance. https://assets.publishing.service.gov.uk/media/5a7c2f73 40f0b674ed20f617/9576-TSO-Health_Visiting_Domestic_Violence_A3_Posters_WEB.pdf

Education Endowment Foundation (EEF) (2024) *A School's Guide to Implementation: Guidance Report*. https://educationendowmentfoundation.org.uk/education-evidence/guidance-reports/implementation

NASUWT (2025) *Community cohesion*. www.nasuwt.org.uk/advice/in-the-classroom/children-and-young-people/community-cohesion.html

NSPCC (2024) Protecting children from domestic abuse. htttps://learning.nspcc.org.uk/child-abuse-and-neglect/domestic-abuse
UN (2023) Achieve gender equality and empower all women and girls. United Nations. https://sdgs.un.org/goals/goal5
UN (2025) The 17 Goals. United Nations. htttps://sdgs.un.org/goals

# 8
# Suggested Lesson Plans and Topics

## Introduction

This chapter explores ways in which to map out your PSHE, computing and wider curriculum, to ensure that ideas of consent, personal space, online safety and healthy relationships are taught throughout early years and primary school. It explores using literacy and books to introduce ideas, smash gender stereotypes and stimulate meaningful discussions around misogyny, feminism and positive masculinities. Starting early by equipping children with the skills to navigate the world will support the elimination of misogyny in school and wider society. The promotion of negative and problematic stereotypes, which children are exposed to everywhere, contributes to existing narratives that undermine and restrict help-seeking – particularly in relation to mental health and wellbeing, and puts women and girls at risk with narratives that normalise harassment and abuse, and promote unhealthy relationships and victim blaming.

## Curriculum *is* Safeguarding

As far as I am concerned, the curriculum *is* safeguarding. Yes, of course, we want to teach a range of skills – reading, writing, maths and other skills and knowledge that will empower children. However, the most important thing we can teach children is how to keep themselves and others around them physically and emotionally safe, and make informed decisions on how to protect themselves and others from harm and abuse. Through the range of curriculum subjects, we have to foster a culture of safety and wellbeing and integrate safeguarding principles into the curriculum. This is done explicitly through subjects like PSHE and RSE but also discreetly through the other subjects – from using extended writing pieces to build empathy with others, to understanding how to calculate and manage money and finances through maths, to learning about taking notice of the physical environment in geography.

Through PSHE, your programme of work must help children understand their personal boundaries, recognising potential risks and how to respond appropriately in different situations. Children need to have opportunities to regularly explore online safety, bullying and relationships, helping students understand the importance of respecting themselves and others – not just one-off lessons once a term or year. In all lessons there must be a recognition of intersectionality, that different people may have different experiences and lessons must promote diversity, equality and respect for others. For example, a wheelchair user might make different informed decisions to keep safe on transport than someone not in a wheelchair – not because they are victims or need saving – but because people have different lived experiences of the same situations and that must be recognised in order to build empathy.

A culture of safeguarding in school starts with the quality of the curriculum – enabling children to develop empathy, use their voice to speak out, learn accountability for their actions and support them to become responsible, resilient and safe individuals.

> Consent education should start early and be included beyond the context of sex, being integrated sequentially at all stages rather than treating it as a checklist exercise. When the reality of sex and relationships is complex, introducing the nuance of consent at such a late stage means it is often too little too late to give young people the knowledge they need and deserve. (Vidyut Chattopadhyay from Sexpression: UK, as quoted in Sex Education Forum, 2024.)

## No Means No

This idea is the essential foundation in developing healthy relationships, body boundaries and addressing sexual harassment. It needs to be taught from the moment children start nursery until they leave statutory education at age 18. The Ofsted report following the *Everyone's Invited* review, which invited young people to disclose problematic behaviours they had experienced in school, right the way up to sexual assault and rape, across the UK, highlighted pupils expressing that they would have benefited from a better and more explicit education about consent and related topics (PSHE Association, 2022). The PSHE Association has detailed guidance on how to teach about consent in primary school, including the law around consent, in an effective, informed and safe way. We must teach children to understand the skills and attributes they need to manage seeking, giving, not giving and withdrawing consent in all different possible contexts, including within friendships and relationships. Learning about consent must be holistic – not just something to be learned academically; it must be covered within the context of broader PSHE learning to support children to apply learning when exploring linked concepts like empathy, mutual respect, fairness, trust, negotiation, communication, risk and personal safety, bullying and abuse.

The DfE's statutory RSHE guidance (DfE, 2019: 21–22) includes what should be covered in key stage 2 in relation to respectful relationships and being safe. These are some of the points:

*Respectful relationships*

- Practical steps they can take in a range of different contexts to improve or support respectful relationships

- That in school and in wider society they can expect to be treated with respect by others, and that in turn they should show due respect to others, including those in positions of authority.
- The importance of permission-seeking and giving in relationships with friends, peers and adults.

*Being safe*

- What sorts of boundaries are appropriate in friendships with peers and others (including in a digital context)
- That each person's body belongs to them, and the differences between appropriate and inappropriate or unsafe physical, and other, contact.

# Definitions (for Teachers)

*Consent* means …

> … agreement that is given willingly and freely without threat, fear or exploitation, by a person who has the capacity to give their agreement.

*Sexual consent* means …

> … a positive choice to take part in a sexual activity by people who understand the nature and implications of the activity they are agreeing to. All parties take part not because they have to, but because they want to. Consent must be free – an active, personal choice; it cannot be inferred, assumed, or gained by coercion or exploitation. The person giving consent must be old enough (see the last bullet point in the list below), have all the information they need to make the decision, and be in a fit state to give consent (and not, for example, with their judgement impaired by alcohol or drugs) (PSHE Association, 2022).

How to know if someone gives consent …

- Look to someone's verbal language and body language
- It must be without ambiguity or confusion as to whether consent has been given
- Just because someone doesn't say no, it doesn't mean that it is consent
- It must be free from threat and must be informed
- They must have the capacity to give consent – for instance, this cannot be given if they are drugged, too drunk or have a learning disability which renders them unsure of what they are consenting to
- The person must be able – legally and ethically – to give consent. The age of consent in the UK is 16 years old, meaning a child under this age cannot legally give consent to sexual activity. The law is designed to protect young people from being abused and exploited. The law is not designed to prosecute under 16-year-olds from engaging in mutually consenting, non-abusive, sexual activity.

*Personal space* means ...

> ... having enough space between you and someone else, meaning you do not feel threatened or uncomfortable.

*Privacy* means ...

> ... having the right to be left alone and have control over your personal information.

## Ground Rules

Great PSHE learning requires well-established ground rules to ensure the learning environment is safe for all. This rule also applies to teaching about concepts linked to consent in other subjects too. These ground rules need to be revisited in each lesson and throughout the lesson, and agreed by all children. A key to this is confidentiality and anonymity.

### Key Ground Rules ...

The PSHE Association (2022) suggests the following:

- *Be non-judgemental.* We do not judge others, put anyone down or laugh at anyone. It is OK to respectfully disagree with someone else.
- *Listen respectfully.* Remind children they are to listen to each other's views and will be listened to when they share their views.
- *Don't make assumptions.* Children should agree not to make assumptions about someone's behaviours, experiences, feelings or values.
- *Be open.* Children should be honest and open, but not *personal* – i.e. no discussions about an individual's private life.
- *Use appropriate language.* Remind children that we use the correct terminology for things, including body parts. No slang to be used, and if it is used, teach children the proper associated word.
- *Seeking advice and help.* Always remind children how and where to get help from if needed, who in school they can talk to if they want to say something and who trusted adults are outside of school.
- *Right to pass.* All children are encouraged to take part in lessons and discussions. However, ensure children know that they have the right to pass on answering a particular question or activity. Always follow up afterwards, one to one, to ensure that the child is OK and/or prompt a discussion with them, letting them know that you are there to listen to them.

## Consent in the Early Years

The idea of consent should be integrated into everyday practice – from modelling boundaries to conversations with children to teaching about seeking permission from others and respecting the answer.

Toddlers love saying 'no!'. Children need to understand what 'stop' and 'no' mean from when they start nursery. This supports children's awareness of body boundaries and physical touch, including knowing they should not touch another person without seeking consent.

Young children must be taught to feel empowered about their bodies. For practitioners, this means asking children for consent for things like hugs, rather than assuming a child wants a hug or to be picked up (which can be easy to do in a nursery). Of course, hugging a nursery child within a classroom is different from a Year 6 say. However, while physical affection or hugging can be beneficial for a child's emotional wellbeing, it is vital that staff maintain professional boundaries and adhere to established policies around body boundaries and find alternative ways to convey warmth and support.

### Tip! 8.1

Try asking a child, 'Would you like a high five or a hug?' This will begin to teach children that they have choice and agency over their bodies. Have visuals for this to support learners who cannot access spoken language.

Ensure that you use the appropriate language and words for parts of the body, not pet names for genitalia, even if this is what a parent might use. Using the scientific words for body parts better protects children, supports avoiding abuse and helps children to talk about things that make them uncomfortable if they ever need to. If you hear a parent use incorrect terminology, speak to them about it. Let them know, 'in our nursery we use the correct words for body parts and here's why …'. Encourage parents to use this language at home too. You could support with an age-appropriate visual where needed. Some adults might feel uncomfortable with this – education is power. Invite them in and listen. Explain that the reason your nursery does this is to keep children safe. Empower them with resources – the NSPCC's PANTS rules and guidance are great for supporting parents in understanding teaching body boundaries in an age-appropriate way.

Children must also begin to learn about *personal space*. In the early years, you can begin to teach children about this by having conversations with children when they stand or sit too close to someone, making them uncomfortable, hug a friend when their friend does not want it, hold someone's hand when they do not want it, bump into others, sit on someone's lap, etc. Some children will struggle with this concept, particularly during times like carpet time, transitions, playtime and lining up. There are lots of things you can do – or you might do already – which teach children about personal space like:

- Using rugs with individual spaces
- Reinforcing with language – 'good lining up', 'good walking', 'good sitting' prompted with Widgit visuals for learners who are unable to access language
- Tell social stories about personal space
- Structure transitions to reduce demands – for example, ensuring a child is at the front of the line or next to an adult for support
- Using visual rewards and praise

> **Tip! 8.2**
>
> Give each child a plastic hoop and say, 'This is your personal space.' If someone comes inside your hoop, they are in your personal space! Play outside holding hoops to see what play feels like with personal space!

## Positive Touch in the Early Years

Children in the early years have lots of opportunities to learn about positive touch, supported by adults. Play like role play, dolls, songs, stories and sensory play can develop children's understanding of touch. Children can learn to soothe, help and nurture. This is an important opportunity to model safe touch, saying 'no' when something is uncomfortable and developing nurturing skills in boys. This is the first step in developing children's understanding of their own bodies and the boundaries of others too – what is appropriate and what's not.

## Surprises vs Secrets and Using Your Voice

From early on, children must learn about how to use their voice to speak out if something feels wrong or not quite right. Children must be taught that if someone does something they are not happy about, they must tell a trusted adult and not keep secrets, even if someone asks them to. They must learn that it is OK and safe to speak with a trusted adult if they meet a stranger who makes them feel uncomfortable, that it's OK to feel that way and that it is safe to speak up and express their feelings. The National Day Nurseries Association advises not to use the term 'secret' in early years classrooms, as it is frequently used by people abusing children. Children must learn about the difference between surprises and secrets. Making a birthday card for a loved one or planning a celebration is a surprise – surprises are things that make people happy and that they will find out about soon. Secrets – or the notion of secrets – can make a child feel anxious or guilty or worried around a loved one (Albert, 2016).

## Working with Parents

Parents play a huge role in teaching about consent and body boundaries – the earlier they do this work the better. Support your parents through workshops, posters and newsletters and remind them that no means no – if a child declines physical affection, let them, it's their right to say no to a hug or kiss or tickling. This includes visitors to homes such as extended family members.

# Consent in Key Stage 1

Moving onto key stage 1, children should further develop their awareness of their own bodies and consent.

## My Body, My Choice

Children must be empowered to deal with unwanted physical contact. They need to be taught the difference in severity of situations, such as what situations may be understood as tricky and what is serious. Children need to be actively encouraged to tell a trusted adult and know about external services such as Childline to get help if they have a serious problem.

Like any skill, it can take time to develop and needs to be regularly practised in different situations in a safe, controlled, age-appropriate way.

In key stage 1, children can be taught to ask before they touch others, what an enthusiastic 'yes' sounds and looks like and how to say 'no' in a clear and firm way. Children can also have opportunities to practise finding out more information to help make an informed decision about whether they want to do something. An example might be, if they were invited to a birthday party, where is it going to be? What activities might they be doing? If it's a footie party, a football lover might give an enthusiastic yes whereas someone who is more into art may say no.

## Touch: Good vs Bad

Teaching about the different types of touch – good, bad and unwanted touch – is a powerful tool, and empowers children if they feel unsafe.

---

### Tip! 8.3

Model clear boundaries about privacy and touch in school, and send firm messages about this through posters, visuals, policies and interactions throughout the day. Many schools have a whole-school approach which includes 'Respect' as part of their school values, and teaching children about their human rights, which alongside effective teaching of PSHE, assists children to practise this value and skill in their daily interactions at school. Giving children plenty of opportunities to develop their oracy, use their voice and explore their own likes and dislikes and how to communicate these clearly, is imperative so they can develop confidence in sharing their boundaries. Give children easy phrases to learn such as 'my body, my choice' so you can start to embed this idea of consent.

## Consent in Key Stage 2

At key stage 2, children will need to continue to develop understanding of healthy relationships and begin to explore the different kinds of relationships there are, boundaries and how important it is to respect the choices and rights of others. They must learn what constitutes a healthy relationship, founded in trust, communication and respect. These ideas must be taught explicitly in PSHE but also integrated into other subjects too. The teaching of consent and modelling this should become part of everyday school life by the time children reach key stage 2. This is building on the foundational learning from key stage 1 and early years.

Children must learn that asking permission is a way of showing respect and making sure everyone feels safe and comfortable.

---

### Tip! 8.4

Everything we do as practitioners is a model for children. Model asking for permission and consent. Things like, 'Can I borrow your pencil please?' or 'Can I show your book to the class?' Give opportunities for children to say no – for example, 'Would you like a high five this morning?' Remember to model saying no to children too – for example, if a child asks for a hug you can say, 'No thank you.'

---

### Role Play

Role play is a key pedagogical approach to use in teaching consent and healthy relationships. Children need to be given real-life scenarios, and role play practising how to face different age-appropriate situations. Practising expressing their boundaries and what they are and are not comfortable with is important, alongside saying no. It is also important that children practise hearing 'no' and accepting it rather than reacting aggressively to it. Children can also practise withdrawing consent.

### Online Safety and Influencers

Online safety needs to be regularly taught through computing lessons and assemblies, in every term rather than just one unit per year. There should be an online safety element to most computing lessons. In fact, I would suggest where possible having two learning objectives to each lesson, one related to the skill and one related to online safety. For example:

- Learning objective: I can debug a problem to identify and fix errors.
- Learning objective: I can explain how to keep safe when using Scratch online.

When learning about influencers, websites or groups and individuals who promote harmful attitudes, avoid naming or showing children content or the websites. If children go home and do a search, it may add to their algorithm, meaning they may be exposed to more and similar content. Remember also not to assume that all children are aware of popular influencers. Some won't be. Again, if you expose children to them, you may be exposing them to attitudes and ideas they were previously unaware of, giving a potentially inspiring role model and affect their future viewing.

> ### Tip! 8.5
>
> Always speak in general terms when referring to influencers and harmful content. This helps children to understand that advice given applies to any problematic influencers they may come across – now or in the future – not just those currently popular and/or causing concern.

## Respecting Privacy

This is particularly important for upper key stage 2, as some children have access to their own phones. The idea of privacy builds on the 'secrets vs surprises' learning from the early years. Privacy means having the right to be left alone and having control over your own personal information. Children need to be taught that everyone has the right to privacy. This can be done through scenarios, giving children the space to think critically about situations and make informed decisions.

An example of a privacy scenario would be:

> Zoe and Frank are friends. After school they like to make dance videos to the latest dance crazes. Zoe asks Frank not to share the video, just to keep it. When Zoe gets home she receives messages from other children in the class saying, 'Love your TikTok video!' Zoe realises that Frank has uploaded their dance video to TikTok.
>
> What should Zoe do?

- Speak to Frank?
- Speak to a trusted adult – in school or at home?
- Report it on TikTok?
- Unfollow Frank?
- Talk to her teacher?

## Metacognition and oracy

> Oracy heightens a community's ability to belong to each other, whilst valuing individuality. It makes every voice matter; these processes are built on the principles of a democratic society. (Apps, 2022)

We've discussed earlier in the book the concept of using conversation, not debate, when dealing with children expressing ideas. Rather than asking children closed questions give them the space, time and opportunity to explore ideas and prompt their oracy with metacognitive sentence starters such as:

- I'm seeing …
- I'm thinking …
- I'm feeling …
- I'm wondering …
- I'm noticing …

In addition, give children the language of exploratory talk – the concept of finding out more about a person's ideas, rather than simply saying something else:

- Building on what you said …
- Can you tell me more about …
- I don't really understand. Can you explain in a different way …
- I like your idea about …

Give children the language of respectful challenge such as:

- I hear you but …
- I'd like to challenge you on …
- Have you considered …

Display these sentence starters in your classroom somewhere visible to all children, ensuring they are adapted for all learners, using visuals where needed. Remember to also model them in your teaching. Developing children's oracy – their ability to express themselves articulately – not only helps to keep children safe, but is also strong equitable practice for disadvantaged groups. When children have the platform to speak, and be listened to, it builds self-worth, making them feel respected, important and that their voice matters.

### Example Planning Sequence

### Upper KS2 White Ribbon project: Anti-misogyny and positive masculinity

White Ribbon is a charity which engages men and boys to end violence against women and girls.
  These sessions are run as a circle time, with the core purpose of:

- Raising awareness about misogyny: spotting it, stopping it
- Developing allyship
- Challenging gender stereotypes

Children work towards achieving a White Ribbon lanyard and badge. In order to do this, they must complete their weekly promises.

## Session 1 Focus: Allyship, Key Vocabulary – Ally, Allyship, Feminist

**Learning objective:** Understand what an ally is and demonstrate allyship behaviour.

**Opening question:** What is an ally? (pair responses)

**Explain:** an ally is someone who supports people/a person who is being discriminated against, even though they do not belong to that group themselves.
Show pictures of Gareth Southgate, Ashley Waters, Tom Hardy, Harry Styles and John Legend.

**Ask:** What do you think they all have in common? Answer: These men are allies to women as they stand up for women's rights.

**Activity:** What are the ingredients for a great ally (e.g. bravery, kindness, care)? Children use flipchart paper to write ideas.

**Challenge:** The best way to stand up for someone is violence. True or false?

**Structure:** Children sit in a circle.

**Resources:** Photos of role models, flipchart paper and felt tips.

**Wider school promise:** To notice others being allies on the playground and give them a shout out on the ally board.

## Session 2 Focus: Consent, Key Vocabulary – Consent, Freely, Threat, Body Language

**Learning objective:** Understand what an ally is and demonstrate allyship behaviour.

**Opening question:** What is consent? (pair responses)

**Explain:** consent is agreeing to let something happen, freely and without threat.

**Explain 123:**

1 Recognise it – 'I understand you said no.'
2 Accept it – 'I accept you said no, I will not ask again.'
3 Process it – 'It's OK for me to feel emotions about it.'

**Ask:** What should happen if consent is not given?

**Ask:** Once someone has given consent, does that consent last forever? (e.g. If someone agrees to lend their friend a pencil, does their friend need to ask again if they want to borrow it again a week later?)

**Challenge:** How can we respond to someone saying no? Get children to share verbally, then share:

- Uncomfortable body language
- Nervous laughter

- Through a friend
- Running away

**Structure:** Children sit in a circle

**Resources:** Scenario cards, such as:

- A group of older children are standing around Andie. They ask them if they can borrow their football. Andie says yes. Is this true consent? Why/Why not?
- Bailey receives ten WhatsApp messages in one night about coming to the park on Friday. Eventually Bailey says yes. Is this true consent? Why/Why not?

**Wider school promise:** Remember 123. When someone says no:

1 Recognise it
2 Accept it
3 Process it

See if you can spot someone struggling with this on the playground and remind them of 123.

## Session 3 Focus: Pressure, Key Vocabulary – Consent, Freely, Threat, Body Language

**Learning objective:** Understand how to respond to pressure.

**Opening question:** If someone keeps asking you a question, should you give in and just say yes?

**Explain:** sometimes we feel pressured to do something. Sometimes it can feel annoying or upsetting to keep saying no.

**Play Myth or Truth.** Say a statement. If children think it's a myth they stand up. If they think it's a truth they sit down. Statements:

1 If you don't do what someone wants you to do you will lose them as a friend. (Myth)
2 Peer pressure only comes from friends. (Myth)
3 Peer pressure comes from media, friends and family. (Truth)
4 Peer pressure comes from a desire to fit in. (Truth)

**Ask:** What advice would you give to someone feeling pressured to do something they didn't want to do? Children share with their partners.

**Challenge:** Let's practise saying 'no!' On a sticky note, write down three different ways to say no. Examples:

- I don't want to.
- No thank you.

- I'd rather not.
- Stop, I don't like it.

Once all children have their sticky note ask children to move around the room. When they encounter each other, one child asks a question - e.g., 'Do you want to come and play?', Do you want to join our WhatsApp group?, Children respond with one of their 'no' responses.

**Structure:** Children sit in a circle

**Resources:** Sticky Notes

**Wider school promise:** Look out for children feeling pressured on the playground. See if you can be an ally to someone struggling.

## Session 4 focus: What does it mean to be a man?
## Key vocabulary - masculinity, non-binary, harmful, gender, stereotypes

**Learning objective:** To challenge the gender stereotypes around men.

**Opening question:** What does it mean to be a man? Gather responses verbally to gauge children's ideas.

**Ask:** If you crossed out the word 'man' and replaced it with 'human', would the ideas be the same?

**Explain:** If someone does not identify as a man or woman, they are called non-binary.

**Challenge:** Get a long roll of paper. Write the words 'a real man' in the middle. At one end write 'positive' and at the other end 'harmful'. All children take a felt tip pen and write words on the roll of paper. Whilst children are writing, give prompts like strong emotional wellbeing, respect for others, self-expression, inclusive. Notice words and prompt discussion responses - What is 'strength'? Does this mean physically strong? What does it mean to be emotionally strong? Ask children to add possible careers and jobs onto the paper - notice any stereotypes and address them. What have we learned about gender stereotypes? Use metacognitive sentence starters to prompt discussion: I'm thinking, I'm noticing, I'm wondering, I'm seeing, I'm feeling.

**Structure:** Children sit in a circle

**Resources:** Roll of paper

**Wider school promise:** Remember, there's no one way to be a man or a woman - and some people don't identify with either!

## Session 5 Focus: What Does it Mean to be a Woman? Key Vocabulary – Femininity, Non-Binary, Harmful, Gender, Stereotypes

**Learning objective:** To challenge the gender stereotypes around women.

**Opening question:** What does it mean to be a woman? Gather responses verbally to gauge children's ideas.

**Ask:** If you crossed out the word 'woman' and replaced it with 'human', would the ideas be the same?

**Explain:** If someone does not identify as a man or woman, they are called non-binary.

**Challenge:** Get a long roll of paper. Write the word 'a real woman' in the middle. At one end write 'positive' and at the other end 'harmful'. All children take a felt tip pen and write words on the roll of paper. Notice words and prompt discussion responses – What is 'beauty'? Ask children to add possible careers and jobs onto the paper – notice any stereotypes and address them. Get out last week's paper about 'What it means to be a man' and compare. Use metacognitive sentence starters to prompt discussion: I'm thinking, I'm noticing, I'm wondering, I'm seeing, I'm feeling.

**Structure:** Children sit in a circle

**Resources:** Roll of paper

**Wider school promise:** Remember, there's no one way to be a man or a woman – and some people don't identify with either!

## Session 6 Focus: Online Friends, Key Vocabulary – Healthy, Safe, Relationships, Red Flags

**Learning objective:** To understand how to keep safe online.

**Opening question:** Do you know how to stay safe and help your friends to stay safe online?

**Ask:** Can we always trust everyone we meet online?

**Explain:** Today we will be thinking about ways to maintain safe, healthy online relationships, as well as the differences between online and offline relationships.

**Challenge:** Play agree, disagree, not sure. Explain that you are going to say some statements. On one side of the classroom stick a sticky note saying 'agree'. On the other side write 'disagree'. In the middle of the room write 'not sure'. Read the statement. Ask children to move to the area of the room which represents their opinion. After each statement, ask a few children to justify their thoughts. Statements:

- It is easier to talk to people online about things that you might be too shy to say to people face to face.
- You can have fun meeting people online.
- You can talk to someone whenever you like, any time of day or night.
- You can be your real self online.
- If you're really into something (e.g. a game), you can find lots of people online who are into the same thing.

Explain that 'red flags' are warnings that there may be a problem or an issue. Read Mo's story:

Mo is 11 years old and has just started secondary school. There were a few children Mo knew who also came from Mo's primary school to this secondary school. However, they are in different classes and it seems they have all made new friends. Mo hasn't made any friends yet and is feeling quite lonely. One weekend, Mo is completing their homework and doing some research online for the topic. They come across a website which seems helpful for homework - people seem to be talking about homework. Mo sets up an account calling it Mo2007 and is chatting with lots of people but ends up chatting mostly with someone called Alex2007 - about homework but also about other things like school and home. Alex2007 says they are the same age as Mo and they seem to give Mo lots of advice about school and homework and feeling lonely. Mo starts staying up late chatting to Mo about lots of things. Sometimes Mo is really tired in the morning, which Mo's mum has noticed. Mo's mum asked if they were not sleeping well. Mo does not tell their mum about Alex. Mo receives a message one day from Alex saying, 'I'm moving to your school next week - we can be real friends. Let's meet up - don't tell your mum cos she won't get it.'

Ask children in small groups to think about the following:

1. What do you think about this story? Use metacognitive sentence starters to prompt discussion: I'm thinking, I'm noticing, I'm wondering, I'm seeing, I'm feeling
2. Is Mo's online relationship healthy and safe?
3. What red flags are there to help you decide? (You could mark these with a highlighter pen)
4. What advice would you give Mo at the end of the story?

**Structure:** Children sit in a circle

**Resources:** Sticky Notes with agree, disagree and not sure, highlighters

**Wider school promise:** Always check with a trusted adult if you are unsure about an online friend. If a friend mentions something that you think is worrying, you can speak to an adult on behalf of your friend. This would be a good ally.

## Other Useful Topics in the Fight Against Misogyny

Let us now explore some other useful topics that we need to bear in mind in our fight against misogyny in schools.

### Body Image, Fatphobia and Body Diversity

> 8% of boys and 14% of girls aged 9–10 had a negative image of their body, with 3% of normal weight boys and 7% of normal weight girls rating themselves as "too fat" … 11% of 13-year-old girls suffer intense worry about getting fat. This compares to 4.7% of boys the same age. (PSHE Association, 2015: 23).

Fatphobia means discrimination against someone based on their weight or 'fatness'. Fatphobia and misogyny are inextricably linked, and are applied predominantly to women as a way to control and judge their bodies and impose patriarchal societal expectations. Whilst also being inherently misogynistic, fatphobia is also deeply rooted in racism, with its roots spanning the transatlantic slave trade where colonists asserted Black people were gluttonous (Strings, 2019). Children experience aspirational thinness and body shaming through media from a young age, and we need to tackle this in school. Look at Disney characters as an example. Fat Disney characters perpetuate fatphobic assumptions and can lead to bullying – fat Disney characters are jolly or clumsy or foolish or aggressive. Some examples are: The Matchmaker in Mulan, Ursula in Little Mermaid and Clawhauser in Zootopia (Sebastian and Sankar, 2023).

Body image is a topic of increasing concern for children. Our culture is infused with constant messages linking self-worth to physical appearance and the growth of social media bringing celebrity culture into children's bedrooms, leaving children and young people feeling 'increasingly besieged by sexualised and unrealistic images of beauty' (PSHE Association, 2015: 4).

Key considerations:

- Build teaching about body image into PSHE – check out Body Happy Org or the PSHE Association for great resources and programmes of study.
- Use inclusive images around the school and in your resources, showing a range of body diversity. This creates a culture of acceptance and representation. Remember to show a range of intersectional identities (e.g. race, disability). Check out Changing Faces – a charity which supports respect for people with visible difference.
- Capture pupil voice – we need to understand how children feel so we can target quality teaching and support.
- Consider your own understanding – do not take part in self-deprecating commentary on your own body and appearance, do not talk about unflattering photos of yourself or others including celebrities, do not talk negatively about your own appearance, do not fat-shame yourself. It is our responsibility to model positive self-talk, especially in front of children and staff.
- Make sure the classroom is a safe learning environment with clear ground rules.
- It's not just a girl's issue – more and more boys are struggling with self-image, especially around ideas of physical strength and the idea that to be a man you need to be tall and muscly, etc.

- Use visitors to the school to support the teaching around body image – it could be the local authority PSHE lead, nurses, charity workers or other external practitioners.
- Seek training and CPD around teaching if you are unsure!

Great books about body positivity:

- *Bodies Are Cool* by Tyler Feder
- *B is for Bellies* by Rennie Dyball and Mia Saine

## Using Disney and Marvel as Teaching Points

Looking at Disney and Marvel characters is a really interesting, accessible and visible exploration into teaching ideas around gender, stereotypes and expectations. These films are jam-packed with gender stereotypes that can be unpicked and discussed in a critical way by children.

Disney princesses have evolved from Snow White and Cinderella who were thin and white, and adhere to traditional ideas of what a girl should be – pretty, obedient and in desperate need to be saved by a knight in shining armour! This moved onto the era with Belle (*Beauty and the Beast*) and Jasmine (*Aladdin*) both of whom are praised for their intelligence. This evolved into Anna and Elsa from *Frozen* showing they do not need saving by men to Merida, Mulan and Moana who provide alternative narratives about women, strength, bravery and independence (Alp, 2021).

Conversely, Marvel movies often depict men in stereotypical roles of aggression, physical strength, ambition, saving and ruling the world (Karma and Bhad, 2023). As an example, you could look at the character of Tony Stark – Iron Man – who demonstrates this idea of hypermasculinity: violent, excited by danger, disrespectful towards women and describes himself as a 'genius, billionaire, playboy, philanthropist' (Šutovská, 2020). You can also look at Captain America and notions of traditional masculinity – the ultimate athlete, a soldier battling to save the world.

### Tip! 8.6

Show children images and clips from the different Disney and Marvel movies as part of your lessons on gender stereotypes. What stereotypes can we see? Ask them to respond using metacognitive sentence stems such as I'm wondering, I'm noticing, I'm feeling.

## Positive Masculinities: Redefining Strength and Vulnerability

Most men don't fall into what social media tells boys they have to be – physical, aggressive and dominant. Teaching boys how to be empathetic and express emotions redefines the concept of strength and the power of vulnerability.

There are some wonderful books which can be used to develop ideas around redefining strength and vulnerability, as well as teaching this explicitly to all children in PSHE lessons, such as:

- *What is Masculinity? Why Does it Matter? And Other Big Questions* by Jeffrey Boatye and Darren Chetty
- The Stories for Boys Who Dare to Be Different series by Ben Brooks
- *Rajiv's Starry Feelings* by Niall Moorjani and Nanette Regan
- *The Noise Inside Boys* by Pete Oswald
- *Quiet is Strength* by Mary Hand Ness and Dow Phumiruk
- *I am a Thundercloud* by Leah Moser and Marie Hermansson

Mentoring is really important – especially for boys who are displaying problematic behaviours. Mentoring is, of course, also powerful for girls and gender nonconforming students too. Of course, children need consequences for poor, aggressive or bullying behaviour, but they also need to learn *why it is* wrong so that they can develop skills to change behaviours.

Think about the boys who often get in trouble at your school. Nationally in 2023/4, the suspension rate for male pupils was more than 1.5 times that of female pupils and pupils with special educational needs continue to have some of the highest rates of suspensions and permanent exclusions (DfE, 2025). If this is also the case in your school – which it is statistically likely to be – think about how you can mentor boys who are struggling effectively. Mentoring is *preventative* work. For example, a boy with ADHD might not know and understand his feelings and thoughts and his neurodivergence. A strategy could be for mentoring to focus on understanding their ADHD, learning about it, learning about how to spot behaviours and feelings as they arise and to use zones of regulation as a way to tackle this. There are some brilliant books that a mentor could use and read with a child to support their development, such as *The Survival Guide for Kids with ADHD* by John F. Taylor and the Neurodivergent Kids series from Jessica Kingsley Publishers.

### Tip! 8.7

Seek male mentors for boys. You may have male learning mentors on your team, or if you don't, look at local organisations and see if you can find someone suitable. Providing male mentors for boys will help to provide a positive male role model, someone who is able to express their feelings and support growth.

## Pupil Voice

Pupil voice and pupils' experiences of the classroom and school can help to form a core element of the school's approach to preventing and responding to misogyny, sexism and sexual harassment. Children could set up their own feminist/equality groups, sharing their ideas in safe learning spaces, encouraging them to grow their understanding and change their behaviours because they recognise gender stereotypes harm them and all their peers.

> ### Tip! 8.8
>
> Just like the leadership team have a school development plan, the school council should have a child-friendly version of this, and in their meetings think about how they can work towards achieving these goals. You may, for example, have a target for developing inclusive practice, so the school council setting up an equality group or campaigning/fundraising for a charity fighting against gender stereotypes or VAWG could be an action related to this target.

## A Note on Adaptive Teaching

It is vital that all learning is accessible to *all learners*, as we know already that intersectional identities and neurodiversity *can* put children more at risk and make them more vulnerable to problematic narratives or to being less able to express and understand their barriers. Teaching *must* be adaptive, use visuals and other scaffolds to support learners. Use the Education Endowment Foundation's five-a-day principle to support children with SEND to succeed:

1 *Explicit instruction.* Model, check frequently for understanding, provide guided practice
2 *Cognitive and metacognitive strategies.* Give opportunities for children to plan, monitor and evaluate learning, supporting the movement of information into long term memory
3 *Scaffolding.* Provide supportive tools to allow every child to succeed – writing frames, visuals, examples
4 *Flexible grouping.* Allocate groups temporarily based on current level of mastery in that topic, subject or skill
5 *Using technology.* Use technology to support learning – for example, a class visualiser, tools to support children to practise or record learning, access and model worked examples, reading pens for dyslexic students, and translated resources (EEF, 2022)

## In Summary …

The work on tackling misogyny in primary school must be done through both explicit teaching, but also discretely across the curriculum. We must address the concept of consent right from nursery and build up throughout the primary year groups, so that children leave school with this idea deeply embedded in their understanding of self and behaviour. We must amplify girls' voices, and the voices of gender nonconforming children from a range of intersectional identities, and mentor boys to make real, sustained change.

## References

Albert, A. (2016) Secrets: Which should you tell and which keep? DayNurseries.co.uk www.daynurseries.co.uk/news/article.cfm/id/1578355/Secrets-cross-my-heart-and-hope-to

Alp, A. (2021) From Snow White to Moana: The evolution of Disney princesses. *The Stanford Daily*. https://stanforddaily.com/2021/08/12/the-evolution-of-disney-princesses

Apps, S. (2022) The power of voice: Oracy as a tool for equity through education. Blog. https://queenstreet.group/the-power-of-voice-oracy-as-a-tool-for-equity-through-education/

Department for Education (DfE) (2019) *Relationships Education, Relationships and Sex Education (RSE) and Health Education*. Statutory guidance for governing bodies, proprietors, head teachers, principals, senior leadership teams, teachers. https://assets.publishing.service.gov.uk/media/62cea352e90e071e789ea9bf/Relationships_Education_RSE_and_Health_Education.pdf

Department for Education (DfE) (2025) Autumn term 2023/24: Suspensions and permanent exclusions in England. https://explore-education-statistics.service.gov.uk/find-statistics/suspensions-and-permanent-exclusions-in-england/2023-24-autumn-term

Education Endowment Foundation (EEF) (2022) EEF blog: The five-a-day approach: How the EEF can support. https://educationendowmentfoundation.org.uk/news/eef-blog-the-five-a-day-approach-how-the-eef-can-support

Karma, A. and Bhad, A. (2023) Disney setting and changing gender stereotypes. *Global Media Journal*, 21, 66. www.globalmediajournal.com/open-access/disney-setting-and-changing-gender-stereotypes.php?aid=94040

PSHE Association (2015) *Teacher Guidance: Key Standards in Teaching about Body Image*. www.ghll.org.uk/Key%20Standards%20in%20Teaching%20about%20Body%20Image.pdf

PSHE Association (2022) KS1–5 Teaching About Consent Guidance. https://fs.hubspotusercontent00.net/hubfs/20248256/Guidance/Documents/Teaching%20about%20consent%20-%20teacher%20guidance.pdf

Sebastian, A. and Sankar, A. (2023) *Fatphobia in Disney Movies: Implications and Imprints on Children's Wellbeing, Ishal Paithrkam*. Available at: https://www.ishalpaithrkam.info/2023/06/fatphobia-in-disney-movies-implications.html

Sex Education Forum (2024) Why is it so important to start teaching about consent and privacy with key stage 1 children? www.sexeducationforum.org.uk/news/news/why-it-so-important-start-teaching-about-consent-and-privacy-key-stage-1-children%C2%A0%C2%A0

Strings, S. (2019) *Fearing the Black Body, The Racial Origins of Fat Phobia*. New York University Press.

Šutovská, M. (2020) Toxic Masculinity in Marvel Films. Thesis. Masaryk University Faculty of Arts Department of English and American Studies. https://is.muni.cz/th/u865d/toxic_masc_mcu_final.pdf

# Appendix
# Further Information and Support

## Introduction

Here are suggestions for further reading and CPD to enhance subject knowledge of areas such as PSHE, computing, violence against women and girls, key safeguarding issues and book lists to fill your reading spaces with!

## PSHE

Here are some resources to enhance your PSHE curriculum, knowledge and training.

### PSHE Association

The PSHE Association is the national body for PSHE education, a membership association and charity supporting teachers and schools with resources, training, advice and guidance.

Suggested reading:

- Addressing misogyny, toxic masculinity and social media influence through PSHE education.
- Teacher guidance: Key standards in teaching about body image.
- Teaching about consent guidance.
- Belonging and community: Addressing discrimination and extremism.

Training:

- Pornography: What and how to teach. This is for KS3 and KS4 but it is well worth doing for primary school DSLs.

### NSPCC

Let's talk about PANTS – resources to help keep children safe from sexual abuse.

## Body Happy Org

A social enterprise which provides resources, products, education and training programmes to promote inclusion, celebrate diversity and nurture acceptance, health and wellbeing in children, and a positive body image.

## This Girl Can

#thisgirlcan is a media campaign to encourage girls and women to take up sports. The main resource is a 90-second video featuring a diverse range of girls and women participating in sports aiming to encourage girls and women to feel they can overcome common barriers and get active. On the This Girl Can website, the advert is broken down into shorts where we can learn about individual participants from a range of intersectional identities.

## NEU (National Education Union)

Check out the NEU's Challenging gender stereotypes in STEM resources – some great lesson plans and assemblies ready to go!

# Computing and Online Safety

Here are some resources to enhance your computing curriculum, knowledge and training. Computing is ever-changing so I imagine even by the time this book is published there will be new threats and new training, but here are some organisations which are keeping up with the moving times.

## UK Safer Internet Centre

An organisation which supports educators, social workers and other professionals working with children to play a key role in supporting children to learn about how to stay safe online.
   Suggested reading:

- Revenge Porn Helpline reports record surge in intimate image abuse reports.
- Project Evolve – a progressive online safety curriculum.

## Internet Matters

An organisation providing research, free lesson plans and further resources to support teaching of online safety and digital literacy.
   Check out:

- Breaking down gender stereotypes.
- Fact-checking AI.

- Tackling online hate.
- Parent presentations.

## CPD and Coaching

Here are some organisations that offer CPD and coaching opportunities.

### NSPCC

There are a range of training courses on the NSPCC website, all of which are brilliant. The NSPCC offers online training or you can book for trainers to come to your school. There are training courses and resources on online safety and safeguarding as well as podcasts, videos and resources which are really useful.

Listen to the podcast:

- Black girls' experiences of sexual abuse.

### Unions: NAHT, NEU and NASUWT

Get in touch with your union and see what training they offer on equality, diversity and inclusion. There are great CPD opportunities available alongside equalities groups where practitioners can get together to discuss key issues and share great practice.

### Diverse Educators Ltd

This organisation promotes, diversity, equity and inclusion in schools through training and support. Their network offers masterclasses, induction sessions, INSET training, conference workshops and keynote speeches. Training can be delivered online, in person or as a pre-recording.

### WomenEd

WomenEd is a global grassroots movement which connects existing and aspiring women leaders in education and gives women leaders a voice in education. It offers a range of training, support, articles and blogs to support practitioners.

## Safeguarding

Contact your local safeguarding training providers to see what training you can organise for the intersectional issues below.

## Adultification Training

Adultification is a key safeguarding issue, recognising racism as an issue which impedes the safeguarding of Black and Brown children and diminishes their human rights. Check out Catherine Rushforth and Associates for quality training on this issue.

## Toxic Trio

The toxic trio in safeguarding is recognised as domestic abuse, mental ill-health and substance misuse. This is viewed as a key indicator of increased risk of harm to children.

## Anti-racism Training Course

There are a number of great organisations which offer this training, with a few being Everyday Racism, The Black Curriculum and the NSPCC. This training is important because the lived experiences of global majority women are different and often more complex.

# Book Lists

Here are just a few suggestions for books to fill your reading spaces with, categorised by key theme.

## Consent

- *Don't Hug Doug* by Carrie Finison and Daniel Wiseman
- *Yes! No!* by Megan Madison, Jessica Ralli and Isabel Roxas
- *It's My Body* by Louise Spilsbury
- *Let's Talk about Body Boundaries, Consent & Respect: Teach Children about Body Ownership, Respect, Feelings, Choices and Recognizing Bullying Behaviors* by Jayneen Sanders
- *C is for Consent* by Eleanor Morrison and Faye Orlove

## Books that Challenge Gender Stereotypes

- *Little Red* by Bethan Woollvin
- *Fantastically Great Women Who Changed The World* by Kate Pankhurst
- *Jabari Jumps* by Gaia Cornwall
- *Hidden Figures: The True Story of Four Black Women and the Space Race* by Margot Lee Shetterly and Laura Freeman
- *Tell Me a Tattoo Story* by Alison McGhee and Eliza Wheeler
- *Morris Micklewhite and the Tangerine Dress* by Christine Baldacchino and Isabelle Malenfant

- *The Boy Who Grew Flowers* by Jen Wojtowicz and Steve Adams
- *Mary Wears What She Wants* by Keith Negley
- *The Lipstick* by Laura Dockrill and Maria Karipidou

There are endless brilliant resources out there, if you just spend a little time searching. Train yourself and your teams. Challenge the status quo. Recognise inequalities and commit to change. Fill your libraries and book corners with books which deliver the message to children – equality for all, be you and express yourself to your heart's desire!

# Index

accountability, 72, 106
accreditation, 99–100
alpha male/chad, 63
Ammann, C., 53
anti-misogynistic culture
    behaviour policies and procedures, 22–25
        teaching moments, 23–24
        trauma-informed practice, 24–25
        vicarious trauma, 25
    leadership, recruitment and whole-school culture, 17–22
        developing future female leaders, 21–22
        equity vs. equality, 19
        flexible working, 18–19
        gender equality vs gender parity, 19
        menopause policy, 20–21
        words matter, 22
    recruitment policies and procedures, 29
    representation of women in leadership, 18
    safeguarding policies and procedures, 25–28
        sexual harassment, 26–28
        White Ribbon Day, 28
anti-misogyny and positive masculinity, 112–117
artificial intelligence (AI), 67–70
    and bias, 67–68
    female role models in coding, 69–70
    tools for teachers, 69
aspirational misogyny, 50–51
auditing
    the curriculum, 9–15
        advice, 10–11
        beyond, 13
        implementation steps, 14
        plan for improvement, 13–15
        questions, 11–12
        test the team's unconscious bias, 11
    feminist curriculum, 44–45
awareness days, 82

#balancetonsaïsaï, xix
Bates, L., xvi

behaviour management, 7–8
beta male/cuck, 63
bias
    and artificial intelligence, 67–68
    gender, 9
    unconscious, 11
Black Lives Matter, xviii
black pill, 63
blue pill, 63
body image, fatphobia and body diversity, 120–121

caring masculinity, 51–52
case study, Iceland, 35–36
Chamorro-Premuzic, 18
charities and organisations, 97–99
    Beyond Equality, 97
    End Violence Against Women, 99
    Galop, 98
    Imkaan, 98–99
    Karma Nirvana, 97–98
    Rape Crisis, 98
    Refuge, 98
    Respect, 98
    Respond, 99
    Southall Black Sisters, 98
    Voicebox, 97
    White Ribbon, 97
    Women's Aid, 98
children, pornography and, 65–66
child sexual abuse, xx
classroom
    amplifying girls' voices within, 42–43
    developing oracy, 42–43
    environment, 7
Code First Girls, 70
coercive control, 94
communication
    parent guide to children about gender, 84–85
    empathy through literacy, 88
    LGBTQIA inclusive teaching, 84–86
    tackling homophobia, 87
community, strength of, 91–92

# Index

consent
   in early years, 108–110
      positive touch, 110
      surprises *vs.* secrets, 110
      working with parents, 110
   education, 106
   in key stage 1, 111–112
      good *vs.* bad touch, 111
      my body, my choice, 111
   in key stage 2, 112–113
      online safety and influencers, 112–113
      respecting privacy, 113
      role play, 112
   metacognition and oracy, 113–119
   useful topics in fight against misogyny, 120–123
      note on adaptive teaching, 123
      positive masculinities, 121–122
      pupil voice, 122–123
critical thinking, 72
curriculum, 7
   events to support, 81–84
      awareness days, 82
      International Men's Day, 83
      International Women's Day, 82–83
      LGBTQIA + History Month, 82
      Neurodiversity Celebration Week, 82
      online safety workshops, 81
      Safer Internet Day, 82
      White Ribbon Day, 82
   is safeguarding, 105–108
   working with parents and carers, 81–84

DART (domestic abuse recovering together), 95
developing oracy in classroom, 42–43
discrimination, defined, xvii
discriminatory language, 23
domestic abuse, 94–95
domestic homicide, xxi
domestic violence, xv

educational psychology research, 7
Education Endowment Foundation (EEF), 14, 58
emotional abuse, 95
emotional literacy
   and regulation, 55–57
   teacher CPD around, 57
empathy, 59, 106
   through literacy, 88
endometriosis, xxii
End Violence Against Women, xv
Enough (Johnson), xx
Equality Act 2010, 91
equity *vs.* equality, 19
Etengoff, C., 3
The Everyday Sexism Project, xvi
evidence base for an audit, 10–11

fatphobia, 120–121
female genital mutilation (FGM), xv
female influencers, 71
femicide, defined, xvii
feminism, 31–32
   defined, xvii
feminist curriculum
   auditing, 44–45
   challenging stereotypes through representation, 32–41
   developing oracy, 42–43
   enabling environments, 43–44
   feminist pedagogy, 32
   strong PSHE, 42
feminist pedagogy, 32
femoid/foid, 63
Firmin, C., 26
*Fix the System Not The Women* (Bates), xvi
forced marriage, xv

gay, defined, 88
gender
   bias, 9
   defined, 85, xvii
   equality, 85
   inequality, 85
   parent talk to children about, 84–85
gender-based violence, xviii
gender dysphoria, defined, 87
gender equality, 85
   *vs.* gender parity, 19
   at home, 86
   talking to children about, 85–86
gender health gap, xxii
gender identity, defined, 87
gender nonconforming, 41
   in history, 41
gender-related homicide, xviii
gender stereotypes, xxiii–xxiv, 6
   within everyday practice, 9
   list of books challenging, 34
   pay as a tool for dismantling, 34–35
   representation, 32–41
      gender nonconforming in history, 41
      in history, 36–39
      of men throughout the curriculum, 40
      thematic history, 38–39
      through text, 32–34
      of trans and gender nonconforming people, 40–41
      of women in science, 39–40
      of women throughout the curriculum, 36
      write matters in, 36
   threat, 9
   types of, 32
      domestic behaviours, 32
      occupations, 32

personality traits, 32
physical appearance, 32
global community, 100–102
global masculinity, 52–53
good *vs.* bad touch, 111
Gorse, S., 22
ground rules, 108
gynocentrism, 63

harassment and stalking, 95
healthy digital diet, 73–75
Henry, B., xix
'honour'-based violence, xv
hyper-masculinity, xxiv
    defined, xvii

Iftikhar, I., 52
incels (involuntary celibates), 62
    culture, xxiii
    defined, xvii
influencers, 70–73
    female, 71
    'pick me' girls, 71
    power of, 71–73
International Men's Day, 83, 84
International Women's Day, 82–84
Internet Matters, xxii–xxiii
intersectional identities, xviii–xix
intersectionality, defined, xvii

Johnson, E., 3
Johnson, H., xx
Jones, K., 23

Kane, N. F., xix

leadership
    recruitment and whole-school culture, 17–22
    representation of women in, 18
Lefevor, T. G., 3
lesbian, defined, 88
LGBT identities, xix
LGBTQIA + History Month, 82
local communities, 93
local council, 96–97
Local Independent Domestic Violence Advocacy (IDVA), 96

Mandela, N., 53
manosphere, 62–65
    children access to, 63
    key teaching points of, 64–65
        caring relationships, 64
        critical thinking, 64
        digital media literacy, 64
        identity and belonging, 64
        oracy, 64
        respectful relationships, 64
        strong relationships and sex education and health education (RSHE), 64
masculinity
    caring, 51–52
    global, 52–53
    understanding and defining, 51–53
Men going their own way (MGTOW), 62
menopause symptoms, xxii
Men's Rights Activists (MRAs), 62
Meredith, C., 26
metacognition and oracy, 113–119
#Me Too Movement, xix–xx
Mevowanou, C., xix
mindfulness, 55
misandry, defined, xvii
misogynistic behaviour and attitudes in society, examples of, 2
misogynistic language, 5–6
misogyny
    children experience of, 2–9
    defined, xvii
    and the media, 4
    in online, 61–65
    and religion, 3
    in schools, 5
    useful topics in fight against, 120–123
        body image, fatphobia and body diversity, 120–121
        note on adaptive teaching, 123
        positive masculinities, 121–122
        pupil voice, 122–123
        using Disney and Marvel as teaching points, 121
Moore's Law, 61
Multi-Agency Risk Assessment Conferences (MARAC), 96

National Day Nurseries Association, 110
Neurodiversity Celebration Week, 82
non-binary, defined, 88
note, 5

online and social media
    artificial intelligence (AI), 67–70
    healthy digital diet, 73–75
    influencers, 70–73
    manosphere, 62–65
    misogyny, xxii–xxiii, 61–65
    pornography, xxiii, 65–66
    safety workshops, 81

parent governors, 79
parent reps, 80
parent–teacher association (PTA), 79–80
patriarchy, 31
    defined, xvii

# Index

physical abuse, 94
physical violence, xvii
'pick me' girls, 71
Pick-up artists (PUAs), 62
pinkification, 4–5
policies, 13
pornography, children and, 65–66
positive masculinity, 51
    anti-misogyny and, 114–119
power of influencers, 71–73
    considering school culture, 73
    curiosity not judgement, 71–72
    engage don't dismiss, 72
    knowing the red flags, 71
    teaching responsible behaviour, 72
    using male allyship, 72
premenstrual dysphoric disorder (PMDD), xxii
premenstrual syndrome, xxii
pronoun, defined, 87
PSHE Association, xvi, 106
Pycroft, H., xviii

rape, xv
    and sexual abuse, 95
recruitment policies and procedures, 29
recruitment processes, 13
red pill, 63
religion, misogyny and, 3
religious institutions, 97
representation
    gender stereotypes, 32–41
    in history, 36–39
    of men throughout the curriculum, 40
    thematic history, 38–39
    through text, 32–34
    of trans and gender nonconforming people, 40–41
    of women in science, 39–40
    of women throughout the curriculum, 36
    write matters in, 36
respectful relationships, 106–107
Rights Respecting Award, 100

SafeLives, xix
Safer Internet Day, 82
Saujani, R., 69
school
    communities, 92–93
    developing positive masculinity in primary, 53–60
school PE, 8
self-awareness
    classroom strategies, 54–55
    developing, 53–55
    in boys, 54
    learning, 54
    teaching, 54

self-care, 57–58
sexism, defined, xvii
sexist language, 6
Sexual Assault Referral Centres (SARCs), 96
sexual harassment, 26–28, 106, xv
sexual violence, xvii
Shaw, C., 69
Smallman, N., xix
specialist response (individualised support), 92
sports, 8
stacy, 63
stalking, defined, xvii
state of women's healthcare, xxii
Staudacher, S., 53
stereotype threat, 9
strength of community, 91–92
strong PSHE, 42
surprises *vs.* secrets, 110
Sustainable Development Goals (SDGs), 100

targeted response (additional support for some children), 92
Tate, A., 51, xxii
teacher, definitions for, 107–108
teaching great communication skills, 58–60
tech-facilitated abuse, 95
thot, 63
TikTok, xxii, 22, 43, 61, 63, 71, 113
toilets, 13
toxic masculinity
    aspirational misogyny, 50–51
    developing positive masculinity in primary schools, 53–60
        classroom strategies, 54–55
        developing self-awareness, 53–55
        developing self-awareness in boys, 54–55
        emotional literacy and regulation, 55–57
        self-care, 57–58
        teacher CPD around emotional literacy, 57
        teaching great communication skills, 58–60
    main facets of, 49
    notion of, 49–50
    understanding and defining masculinities, 51–53
transgender, 41
    defined, 87–88
Traoré, B. M., xix
trauma-informed practice, 24–25
Two-Spirit, 41
    identity, 52

UK Feminista Award, 100
uniform policy, 13
universal response (focus on prevention and for all children), 92
University of Kent, 61

VAWG forums, 94
vicarious trauma, 25
violence
    defined, xvii
    against women
        case, xx–xxi
        national context of, xx–xxi
Violence against women and girls (VAWG), xv
visible diversity in school displays, 13
#vraiefemmeafricaine ('real African woman'), xix

White Ribbon Award, 100
White Ribbon Day, 28, 82
wider community events, 13
Widgit, 56
Wojcicki, S., 70
woman, defined, xvii
words matter, 22
working with parents and carers, 77–89
    behaviour incidents, 89
    communication, 84–88
    curriculum, 81–84
    engaging dads and male family members, 88–89
    mattering, 79
    parent–teacher association (PTA), 79–80
    proactive parents, 77–79
    ways of communicating with parents and families with English not as first language, 78
working with wider community, 91–102
    accreditation, 99–100
    charities and organisations, 97–99
    global community, 100–102
    local communities, 93
        gender-based violence incident, 94
        local school nursing services, 95–96
        police, Walk, Talk and Do, 96
        supporting children experienced domestic abuse, 94–95
    local council, 96–97
    religious institutions, 97
    school communities, 92–93
    strength of community, 91–92

YouTube, xxii

zones of regulation, 55–56

www.ingramcontent.com/pod-product-compliance
Lightning Source LLC
Chambersburg PA
CBHW051352070526
44584CB00025B/3730